Fc

How very proud you rw.. e !

inscribed/signed

Strawberries in Wintertime

Wishing you and yours
Strawberries in all
Seasons!

Warmest regards,

Woody Woodburn

FIRST EDITION
Kickstarter Supporter

"Giving does not empty your hands,
it prepares them to be filled."
– Gregory Ansel Woodburn

———

For the giving of their well wishes and generous financial
support in making Strawberries in Wintertime
a reality, I hope these dear friends' own hands
are soon filled many times over.

"MVP" Level Patrons

Kathy and Wayne Bryan
Mike and Bob Bryan

"Manuscript VIP" Level Patrons

Kymberly and Rhett King
Dallas and Greg Woodburn

"Back Cover VIP" Level Patrons

Mary Lou and Gene Paschal
Doreen and Joe Piellucci
Tavis Smiley
Stephenie and Mark Thomas
James Woodburn II

FIRST EDITION
Kickstarter Supported

"Patrons in Print" Level Supporters

Grace and Duane Clark
Ann and Jim Cowan
Nancy and Richard Francis
Mitch Gold
Randi and Scott Harris
Deborah and Joe Hocamp
Mark Jasper
Weenie and Bobo McDougal
Linda and Jerry Mendelsohn
The Mensendiek Family
Joanie and Moustapha Abou-Samra
Annapurna and Ramesh Nori
Robbyn and Frank Paschal
Kathy and Howard Reich
Jo and Chuck Spence
Laurie and Laszlo Tabori
Laura D. Valdez
Debbie and Tim Warren
Cheryl and Brian Whalen
Angie White and Family
Elinor and Joe Wilson
Jodi and Mark Wilson
Caryn and Doug Woodburn

First Edition, 2016
Indie Published by Woody Woodburn
woodywoodburn.com

Also by Woody Woodburn

Wooden & Me: Life Lessons from My Two-Decade Friendship with the Legendary Coach and Humanitarian to Help "Make Each Day Your Masterpiece" (CreateSpace, 2013)

Raising Your Child To Be A Champion In Athletics, Arts and Academics (Kensington Publishing/Citadel Press, 2004) co-authored with nationally renowned coach Wayne Bryan

The Pirate Collection: A Decade of Dominance by Ventura College's Men's Basketball Team (Indie Published, 1995)

Behind the Book

Front cover painting *Strawberry* oil on gesso by British artist Julian Merrow-Smith, who now lives in the South of France. This cover art was a strawberries-in-wintertime experience for me because after seeing Julian's painting on his website (shiftinglight.com) in January 2015, I reached out by email and to my great surprise and gratitude he kindly gave me permission to use it.

———

Interior design, font choices, and layout, as well as the concept and draft of the front and back covers, by the multi-gifted Greg Woodburn.

———

Print-ready creation of the front and back covers was by the immensely talented Dianna Chrysler, a California-based artist, who earned her BA in Studio Arts from the University of Southern California in 2013. Post graduation, Dianna has worked as a freelance designer and photographer, production assistant, and spent her summers working as an instructor for the Idyllwild Arts

Summer Program. She spent the first twenty-four years of her life in Los Angeles, and is currently transitioning to living and working in the San Francisco Bay Area. For more information, please visit: d-chrysler.com.

———

Editing of the manuscript by Dallas Woodburn and Greg Woodburn. For more information about Dallas, and her charity work, please visit: dallaswoodburnpr.com and writeonbooks.org. For more information about Greg, and his charity work, please visit: gregwoodburn.com and giverunning.org.

Contents

———

Dedication

——

For those warm souls who, through their kind words and sweet actions, produce strawberries in wintertime for others in all seasons.

For, as ever, Lisa, Dallas and Greg—the three warmest, kindest, sweetest souls imaginable.

"Make each day your masterpiece."
– John Robert Wooden

———

"Every day is a once-in-a-lifetime experience."
– Gregory Ansel Woodburn

Introduction

——

IN my boyhood, I fondly remember picking wild blackberries and sweet raspberries on humid summer days spent at our family's cabin weekend retreat in rural Ohio. My two older brothers, younger sister, and I filled pail after pail with ripe berries—and nearly as many berries went directly into our mouths before making it into the pails.

So plentiful were the blackberries, especially, that my dad made wine with them. Once. Not only did the blackberry wine prove undrinkable, Mom's favorite pots and pans were stained purple beyond ruin in the process.

Still, wild blackberries and raspberries, and store-bought strawberries, in summertime were always a delicious treat. Too, an expected one.

Berries in the wintertime, in the Midwest, are something I cannot recall from my youth. I am sure they were available at the supermarket in the 1960s for a premium, but Mom never brought them home. The sweetest wintertime fruit we enjoyed were grapefruit and oranges, each individually wrapped in tissue paper inside a large gift box, that my Aunt Shirley sent us from Florida every Christmas.

So it was a magical winter indeed when my family took a Christmas vacation to Ventura in Southern California in 1971 and spent a week at the charming beach house of dear friends of my dad. I had never before seen the ocean in person, much less bodysurfed and built sandcastles; explored tidal pools at low tide and chased a "grunion run" under a full moon's high tide. And here is something else magical: fresh strawberries in wintertime!

Instead of by the bucketful as with Ohio blackberries, we enjoyed Southern California strawberries by the "flat"—a topless box that holds a dozen plastic pint baskets. Additionally, an extra pint was piled high atop a full flat purchased directly from a farmer's market roadside stand. The drive from the stand back to the beach house was too tempting; in the car, en route, I ate strawberries the size of crabapples by the handful, by the big mouthful, sweet nectar dripping down my chin. As with fresh-picked blackberries, my belly happily ached.

I am only guessing, but I imagine the price for an entire heaping-high flat direct from a farmer's stand in Saticoy just outside Ventura—for this area was then, and remains today, the nation's leading producer of strawberries—was probably similar to the cost for two small pint baskets in a Midwest grocery store in December.

The following summer we moved from Columbus to Ventura and strawberries became a year-round fare. Still, in my mind they have always remained a special treat in wintertime. Hence the title of this collection of essays—I hope each one will make you smile and want another.

A note about the format of *Strawberries in Wintertime*. Originally, I arranged the essays in groupings of similar themes as is the general method in this genre. However, editing the pieces while listening to music one evening, I was inspired to rearrange the stories like an album where an artist purposely varies the tempo and lyrical style from one song to next in an effort to create an overarching flow.

So have I tried to do. To be sure, some essays of similar theme simply begged to be placed together in pairings or small clusters, as with the handful about my excursion to Ireland to learn more about my distant family roots. For the greater part, however, I have strived to weave together groupings of four or five dissimilar essays that still flow from one to the next, and then three or four more, over and again. The end effect, I hope, is similar to a set of pleasant waves, much like those I enjoyed as an eleven-year-old boy at play in the Pacific Ocean for the first time. Furthermore, these essays about Life, Love and Laughter— even the few about Loss—aim to warm your heart.

"Live in the sunshine, swim the sea, drink the wild air," advised Ralph Waldo Emerson, who in my mind should have added, "and eat strawberries in wintertime."

One

Firsts and Lasts

———

WE love firsts. First place. First in line. First downs. Perhaps most of all, we love first times.

Especially new parents, who are constantly experiencing firsts. Baby's first smile. First words. First steps.

First, first, first.

In truth, the firsts never stop. Like chocolates on the conveyor belt in the classic episode of *I Love Lucy*, the firsts keep coming. First day of kindergarten, first bike ride, first time driving.

First, first, first.

Sometimes, however, I think we focus too greatly on firsts. Partly this is because firsts are easy—not always easy to accomplish, mind you, but rather easy to recognize.

Your son has never ridden a bike without training wheels—or your hand holding the seat to steady it from behind—and now he does. *Let's go to Ben & Jerry's to celebrate!*

Your daughter scores her first goal in soccer. Another recognizable milestone. *Do you want your Rocky Road in a cone or a cup, Honey?*

We all have our own personal conveyor belt of firsts. First roller-coaster ride, first kiss, first marathon. Again, all easy to recognize and store away in your mental scrapbook.

But what about lasts?

I got to thinking about this over the holidays when my daughter, home from grad school, was listening to Taylor Swift sing "Last Kiss" with the lyric: "Never thought we'd have a last kiss."

It suddenly struck me: I never thought there would be a last time I read my daughter a bedtime story or a last time I gave my son, also home from college for Christmas break, a piggyback ride to bed.

While I can vividly remember composite scenes of reading "Goodnight Moon" and carrying a sleepy boy hugging my neck up the stairs, I cannot specifically remember the *last* time I did either.

Lasts. Lost and forgotten. How sad—we rarely recognize a last while it is happening and miss the chance to press the "record" button on our mental DVRs.

I wish I could specifically remember the last piggyback ride my father gave me. Or the last time my mom held my hand crossing a street. The last time I went fishing with my grandpa.

Lasts, lasts, lasts. Lost, lost, lost.

When was the last time I gave my son and daughter baths in the tub? Had I known it was the last time, wouldn't I have memorized all the details? Splashed a little more and laughed louder at the wet mess?

When was the last time I brushed their teeth for them? Read them Dr. Seuss? Played "Sam the Alligator Man" with them while wrestling on the floor? When was the last time I helped them tie their shoes; helped them assemble a new toy; helped them with homework? As we sing "Auld Lang Syne" to another year gone by and fondly remember long-ago firsts, with the new year arriving and all the firsts it promises to deliver, it seems a fitting time for all of us to make a resolution to pay more attention to lasts.

You remember your child's first wobbly bike ride as you ran alongside, but do you remember the last time you went riding with your dad? Or mom? Or brother or sister, for that matter?

You remember your very first kiss, surely, but do you remember the last kiss with your first sweetheart?

Even kissing your spouse, there will be a last time —but you likely will not know it at the moment. *"Never thought we'd have a last kiss."*

Singing, or thinking, about lasts can seem

melancholy and yet the great thing about lasts is that, unlike firsts, you can have more than one last. Just go do something again and it suddenly becomes a new last.

Since I cannot remember the last time I read "The Runaway Bunny" to my daughter, I need only read it to her tonight—even if she is now twenty-eight years old.

A new last piggyback ride for my twenty-six-year-old son will be a little more challenging—and probably require a couple aspirin afterwards. First, however, I have to wait for him to return from his second humanitarian trip to Africa. I hope he savors every moment there as though it is his last visit.

After all, you never know.

Two

Hello and Goodbye

——

" **A** stranger," Will Rogers said, "is just a friend I haven't met yet."

Three years ago, Jongsoo was a stranger to me. And then we met, crossing paths at the Ventura Aquatic Center community park. I was on my daily run going one direction around the soccer fields and he walked, aided by a cane, in the opposite. "Hi," I said as we passed.

"HELLL-OHHH!" Jongsoo replied in all capital letters with the "o" drawn out and punctuated with an exclamation mark.

Jongsoo greeted me with "HELLL-OHHH!" whenever I saw him in the days and months that followed, often a few times a week, singing it with the same enthusiasm on each ensuing loop, sometimes a dozen times in one afternoon, as if every encounter was the first.

Soon we were exchanging a hug with the day's first "HELLL-OHHH" and high-fives with each ensuing one. Jongsoo's carbonated joy always added a lightness to my stride and heart.

Too, he made me laugh. For one thing, Jongsoo often walked with an old Walkman-sized transistor radio, sans earphones, blaring loud enough to make birds scatter. Moreover, he sometimes did a few dance steps for my amusement.

The sight of Jongsoo and me trying to converse had to amuse all who saw us, an odd couple to be sure: he two decades older; me a foot taller; and neither of us understanding much of what the other was saying despite our exaggerated pantomimes.

One day early on, Jongsoo was limping more than usual and through gestures I asked about his leg. He answered by displaying a scar that looked like a great white shark had taken a bite out of his hip and thigh. Through charades it became clear the "shark" had been a car.

One afternoon, along with a "HELLL-OHHH," Jongsoo gave me a note, in English, explaining he was leaving in five days and would not return for at least a year.

"Thanks for cheering me up whenever I see you at the park," it also read. "Thank you for being my friend."

The following afternoon I handed Jongsoo a return note of thanks with some questions about him. One, two, three days passed and I did not see him at the park. I feared I would not get to say goodbye to my friend.

Why had I not realized sooner that Jongsoo must be living with someone who could translate for us? Mad at myself, I recalled what sports writer Frank Graham once wrote about Bob Meusel, a gruff outfielder with the New York Yankees who in his fading playing days warmed up slightly: "He's learning to say hello when it's time to say goodbye."

On the final day before Jongsoo would fly back to his homeland in South Korea, as I was nearing the end of my run and about to leave the park, a black VW Beetle honked and pulled into the parking lot. Jongsoo had insisted his daughter, Kim, drive him over one last time in hopes of catching me.

"HELLL-OHHH!" Jongsoo sang.

"*An nyoung!*" I said back, after asking Kim for the Korean translation.

From Kim I learned that her father is seventy-six years old, has three children and his arranged marriage is closing in on its golden anniversary. He has been staying in Ventura with Kim, who came to American in 1994 to earn a doctoral degree in Special Education and remained here to teach, and her husband Cory, a software engineer.

I also learned that a taxi had struck Jongsoo five years ago in Seoul; his hip socket and part of his shattered femur needed to be replaced. How he now walks for one to two hours daily is remarkable and inspiring. Surgery and

11

chemotherapy for colon cancer also did not slow him down for long.

After giving my friend a hug, I asked Kim how to say goodbye in Korean.

"*An nyoung!*" I said again, for the salutation, she explained, is the same going as arriving.

I learned to say hello when it was time to say goodbye—but now I will be ready to say hello when goodbye ends and Jungsoo and I meet again at our favorite park.

Three

Summer Memories Jar

———

DESPITE what some who know me might claim, I am not losing my marbles.

In truth, I am gaining them.

And for this I owe a debt of great gratitude to a teacher I had who interrupted his discussion of Shakespeare's *A Midsummer Night's Dream* one afternoon four decades past and shared a personal story. A philosophy, really.

Mr. Hawkins, my fifth-grade teacher, explained he had a jar—importantly, a sizeable pickle jar—on his dresser. Every time something wonderful happened in his life, he would drop a marble inside. A shiny penny would serve the same purpose, he further allowed. His goal was to fill the jar to overflowing by the end of his lifetime. He said he figured—and hoped—he was only about halfway there on both counts.

All these years later, I can only quote a few lines from *A Midsummer Night's Dream* from memory—"Lord, what fools these mortals be!" and "My heart is true as steel"—but I have collected a lot of marbles. I imagine and hope Mr. Hawkins' teaching legacy includes hundreds of jars on dressers filled with tens of thousands of marbles and pennies that have long ago lost their shine, but not their meaning.

In filling my own jar I have come to notice something: summertime is marble time.

As my wise teacher insisted, something need not be monumental—such as winning the Pulitzer Prize or Wimbledon; getting married or getting The Big Promotion; becoming a parent or grandparent—to be deserving of a marble. In fact, oftentimes the simple pleasures are enough.

Simple summer pleasures such as:

Gazing at the stars that always appear brighter on a warm midsummer's night.

A sweet summer romance.

Catching fireflies, catching frogs, catching "running" grunion under moonlight.

Running in the sprinklers.

Running your first marathon—or first 5K.

Running after the ice cream truck.

Enjoying a Popsicle or ice cream cone that tastes better, and colder to your tongue, on a hot summer afternoon.

Sleeping in a tent, be it in the backyard for a

slumber party or in the wild on a camping trip.

Visiting any National Park. Or ballpark.

Going to a baseball game—Little League to Major League.

Hiking to the top of Yosemite Falls.

Climbing Mount Whitney.

Climbing a tree more lovely than a poem.

Writing a poem, or painting a picture, of which you are proud.

TP-ing a friend's house.

Skinny dipping for the first time. Or most recent time.

An afternoon at the beach.

Watching—really watching—a Pacific sunset more beautiful than anything on display in the Louvre.

Wading in the tide pools.

Collecting seashells or building a sandcastle.

Daydreaming while gazing off the pier.

A sailboat trip.

The long drive to a family vacation that, as the years pass, becomes more magically memorable than the destination.

Going fishing and bringing home nothing more than a sunburn and a smile and a tall tale about the one that got away.

Teaching your child to ride a two-wheeler—doesn't

this *always* happen during the summertime?

Spending a week at your grandparents' house and hearing stories about what your mom or dad was like as a child.

Attending your high-school reunion.

Attending a wedding—not just yours, anyone's.

Watching Fourth of July fireworks.

A barbecue with good friends is always better in the summertime.

Playing kick-the-can (Millennials, ask your parents) until your parents holler for you to come inside for the night. Kids today should start playing KTC again.

Evening walks hand-in-hand with your spouse/partner/girlfriend/boyfriend/child.

Riding a merry-go-round or Ferris wheel at the county fair with your child/boyfriend/girlfriend/ partner/spouse.

Whether you are six or ninety-six, you will very soon have one less summer left in your lifetime. *"Lord, what fools these mortals be!"* You can either be melancholy about this or you can rejoice and eagerly make a point of noticing —and savoring—some marble moments.

Four

A Race (and Life) Well Run

—

AN old Irish proverb came to mind last Sunday afternoon in a Southern California hotel ballroom:

'Tis better to buy a small bouquet / And give to your friend this very day,

Than a bushel of roses white and red / To lay on his coffin after he's dead.

Nearly 200 people traveled near and far, not with bushels of roses but rather to give small bouquets, in a manner, to their friend, Laszlo Tabori, who at age eighty-three is very much alive and well.

Specifically, they came to celebrate with him the sixtieth anniversary of the very day—May 28, 1955—when the Hungarian-born Tabori became the world's third person to run a sub-4-minute mile.

His official time was 3 minutes 59 seconds flat, four-tenths faster than Roger Bannister's historic first the previous May. Tabori's feat is proudly recorded on his personalized California license plates: 359IN55.

IN56 a year later at the 1956 Summer Olympics in Melbourne, Tabori—then the world-record holder at 1,500 meters (3:40.8)—finished fourth, a tick away from standing on the medals platform, in the 1,500 and placing sixth in the 5,000. This, despite losing priceless training time and fitness because of the tumultuous Soviet invasion of Hungary.

Directly after the Closing Ceremonies, Tabori defected to America and settled in Southern California near Los Angeles. He remained a star on the world running stage, yet could not compete in the 1960 Rome Olympics because he was a man without a country, as his U.S. citizenship had not yet come through.

Tabori unlaced his racing spikes in 1962 and quickly became a world-renowned distance coach, employing his diabolical interval workouts to train a handful of Olympians, a marathon world-record breaker, two Boston Marathon champions, and myriad collegians at L.A. Valley College and the University of Southern California.

Too, the longtime Oak Park resident created the San Fernando Valley Track Club where he continues to coach men and women runners of non-elite abilities.

Now. Tabori, in 2015, is on his eighty-fourth trip around the sun, but it was those four orbits around a cinder track sixty Mays past that put him in the history books and gave reason for this anniversary party.

And so, one by one, some of his protégés took the microphone and shared stories about how their lives were impacted by this demanding old-school coach with an accent thicker than the spine on his new 290-page autobiography, *Laszlo Tabori: The Legendary Story of the Great Hungarian Runner*.

They talked about his legendary toughness, but also his tenderness. Through laughter they teased him and through tears they called him their hero, cheerleader, mentor, and friend.

Midway through the celebration, the ballroom lights went down and a video went up on a big screen. Instantly it was 1955 again, May 28 again, and Laszlo Tabori was twenty-three again. He did not need a cane due to a hip replacement and his now-white hair was dark and thick and curly. His face was chiseled, his legs sinewy and powerful, and in the grainy black-and-white film footage he was flying around the chalk-lined oval inside London's White City Stadium.

His stride was graceful as poetry as he roared through the backstretch of the fourth-and-final lap, in third place, on the outside shoulders of Britons Chris Chataway and Brian Hewson.

Suddenly, Tabori did precisely what he would tell my son during Greg's recent four years at USC and all the other runners he has coached over the past half-century to do during workouts and races—"Put the guts to it!"—and the kid with No. 9 pinned to his racing singlet overtook Chataway, and then Hewson too, and pulled away to win by five meters. 359IN55.

The ballroom erupted in cheers as if the feat had just happened live.

"That race was a lifetime ago, but I still remember it like yesterday," Tabori later told me, in a private moment, as I thanked him for the important role he has played in my son's life. He added with a twinkle: "I'm happy I'm still around."

After the video ended and the lights came back on and it was 2015 again, the former fastest man in the world slowly made his way to the front of the room and emotionally thanked everyone for showing up.

In truth, everyone was there to thank Laszlo Tabori for showing up in their lives.

Five

A Happiest Place on Earth

DRIVING someone to the airport, especially when it is for a departure flight, always brings to my mind the closing scene in *Casablanca* when Humphrey Bogart, playing Rick, famously bids goodbye in the fog of night to Ingrid Bergman:

"Ilsa, I'm no good at being noble, but it doesn't take much to see that the problems of three little people don't amount to a hill of beans in this crazy world. Someday you'll understand that. Now, now. Here's looking at you, kid."

A pick-up, especially at Burbank's Bob Hope Airport, also reminds me of *Casablanca* because that is where the classic closing scene was filmed—or so legend had it.

Now, now, Ilsa, that noble myth has been busted. Warner Bros. studio archives have been uncovered revealing that the airport footage not shot on a sound stage was actually taken at Van Nuys Airport. This truth is almost as heartbreaking as Bogart sending off his great love.

I prefer the myth when I find myself at Burbank Bob Hope. TSA lines don't mean a hill of beans compared to goodbye hugs and farewell waves.

Disneyland claims to be "The Happiest Place On Earth" but this is another Southern California myth because an airport arrival gate is even more so.

While I loathe waiting for red stoplights and grocery checkout lines and doctor appointments that always seem hopelessly behind schedule, I like to arrive early at the airport to give myself time to wait—and watch.

Watch young couples reunited and old couples, too, because the joy exhibited by both is more contagious than the flu.

Watch children run into their parents' embrace. And grandparents quicken their shuffle to get a hug from their grandchildren.

Watch men give flowers to their loved ones and women give balloons to theirs.

Watch soldiers in uniform lift a child in one heroic arm and a wife in the other, and also lift the spirits of everyone around because of their brave service.

Watch taciturn countenances, weary from waiting, perhaps for a flight delayed, finally glimpse a special face and light up with 100-watt smiles—and those arriving faces, wearier from a long day of travel, beaming back.

I imagine my own face lit up a couple nights ago when the special face I was waiting for finally walked through the arrival doors at Bob Hope Airport; my daughter's face in turn shined as golden as the bouquet of sunflowers, her favorite, I held.

Moments before our reunion, I witnessed a scene worthy of a Hollywood lens, a uniting that began with running squeals of delight and ended in a minute-long embrace. All eyes looked up from their smartphones' texts and emails to watch and smile and even tear up themselves.

The two girls, each in her early teens, appeared to be sisters who had been separated for many months. Or, perhaps, they were close childhood friends now living distantly. To be sure, they disproved Robert Louis Stevenson's belief: "To travel hopefully is a better thing than to arrive."

I was moved and curious, but did not wish to intrude. As fortune would have it, however, the arriving girl had been on my daughter's connecting flight. And so, as we all waited at the luggage carousel, I asked her, "Are you sisters?"

"No, BFFs," came the reply, teen girl talk of course for Best Friends Forever.

Then their story became even more wonderful,

because the arriving girl did not mean "Forever" as in the past but rather into the future. You see, this was the first time the two had actually met in person.

The arriving girl, despite being a casting director's dream of a beach blonde "California girl," was actually from Kansas City, Missouri, while the shorter redhead was a Cali native from the Los Angeles area. They "met" and became BFFs in the 21st Century version of being pen pals via Facebook, Instagram, email and texting.

Their itinerary over the upcoming two weeks, the L.A. redhead said, included all of the "Hollywood things" and the beach... and, of course, the blonde from Kansas City excitedly added, "Disneyland!"

With apologies to Mickey Mouse and friends, *THIS is "The Happiest Place on Earth"* I thought of the airport arrival area, although I did not say it aloud. Instead, I wished the two BFFs a great time. *Here's looking at you, kids.*

Six

First Day of School Tears

———

WHEN it comes to saying hello to a new school year, the words of 19th Century French novelist Jean-Baptiste Alphonse Karr seem perfectly apropos: *"Plus ca change, plus c'est la meme chose."*

"The more things change, the more they remain the same."

On her very first "first" day of school, at Ventura's TLC Preschool (the teaching staff makes the initials stand for Tender Loving Care as well as Trinity Lutheran Church), my three-year-old daughter cried when I dropped her off in the classroom. In fact, it was a full ten minutes before she was finally able to release me from her tight, sobbing hug.

While our morning goodbyes slowly grew from tearful to cheerful as the school year progressed, the first day of TLC the following school year was once again a messy runny-nosed red-eyed event.

Her first day of kindergarten at Poinsettia

Elementary School was barely easier. Fighting to hold back her tears with all her little-girl might, she failed.

Plus ca change, plus c'est la meme chose.

Her first day of first grade was tearless, but certainly not fearless. Second grade was a little easier still; her first day at Cabrillo Middle School better yet; and the first day of her senior year at Ventura High was a happy cakewalk, but...

... Plus ca change, plus c'est la meme chose.

On her first day at the University of Southern California, or rather Move-In Day, my then-18-year-old freshman daughter once again became a three-year-old preschooler. Instead of "USC" emblazoned on her new sweatshirt, it could have read "TLC." The only one who shed more tears was her mom, although she surprised even herself by making it all the way down the long dorm hallway with her back turned before the salty floodgates released as she rounded the corner out of our daughter's sight.

To my credit, I maintained my composure even longer. For a few seconds, anyway. My mistake was pausing to turn and look back, hoping to see an empty doorway and thus knowing my daughter was inside her room having happily begun her college life. Instead I saw her still standing in the hallway waving at me. Her face was woebegone and wet, her eyes red and puffy, her nose running—and never have I seen her look more beautiful, unless it was on the first day of school when she was three or four or five.

Plus ca change, plus c'est la meme chose.

Do not be mistaken by her homesick hugs; my daughter is strong and confident and accomplished and embraces adventure. She has traveled extensively and studied abroad three times. She loves arriving at new places; it is just she also hates leaving familiar old ones.

She has always been world-class at hellos and lousy at goodbyes—and, truth is, this is a lovely quality. Her tight hugs of greeting make one feel deeply loved; her wet hugs upon parting somehow even more so.

Things change. Instead of a school bus, my daughter took an airplane on her way to her final "first" day of school at Purdue University for her third and final year of its M.F.A. Creative Writing Program.

Things stay the same. Near the entrance to get into the long security line at the airport it was a full ten minutes until she was finally able to release me from her tight, sobbing goodbye hug. A couple times over the years we have tried the get-it-over-with-quickly Band-Aid approach with a hurried hug-and-go, but this causes more tears, not fewer. And so we linger, aging father and Daddy's Little Girl Always.

After we eventually parted and I walked away a

short distance down the terminal hallway, I did what I have always done, still do, and always will: I turned around for one final look at her. I cannot resist. Usually she is well into the security line by then and can only smile and wave.

But this time she was not yet trapped in the line. A grandmotherly woman watching the scene unfold said aloud, not unkindly: "Rookie mistake. Never look back."

I disagree. I got to look back at my beautiful twenty-five-year-old daughter and see her age three again as she rushed back to give me one last wet-and-wonderful first-day-of-school hug.

Plus ca change, plus c'est la meme chose.

Seven

Friendly Advice is Golden

———

"WHEN the student is ready," a Buddhist proverb states, "the teacher will appear."

Or, as I happily experienced the other day, sometimes the wise friend appears.

In this case, he showed up at Happy Hour. While the chips, salsa, guacamole and micro-brews were enjoyable, most appetizing of all—as usual with Scott—was the conversation. Scott Harris belongs on a mountain peak, sitting cross-legged, rubbing his bearded chin in contemplative thought.

My friend is a Renaissance man. He runs his own highly successful business, yet favors flip-flops to wingtips. His interests include literature (he reads more than one-hundred books a year) and music (plays a killer harmonica) and travel (is well on the way towards one of his bucket-list goals of visiting every U.S. national park).

But what I most admire about Scott is he is a role model of a family man. Happily married for three decades, he has helped raise two amazing children. Importantly, Scott remains as close to his adult son and daughter now as when they were learning to ride two-wheelers.

Our conversation turning from travel to fatherhood, I asked Scott to share his magic formula. His parenting mission statement: "I made my kids my priority and always made time for them."

My remarkable friend then remarkably noted, matter-of-factly without a trace of conceit, that he only missed one of his daughter's equestrian events when she was a national-class youth competitor. And of more than one thousand baseball games his son played in, Scott was absent from a mere two. That's a hall-of-fame batting average.

I felt a kinship as my son ran in perhaps five hundred races—from youth cross-country and track meets through high school and four years of college competition in both sports—and I similarly missed only two.

And my track record for my daughter's sports and drama events was without a blemish—but only for another twenty-four hours, I confided to Scott.

I shared how my daughter played the lead of Dorothy in an elementary school play and, despite having already attended the dress rehearsal, I skipped covering two Lakers playoff games during the Magic Johnson "Showtime" Era to be at Opening and Closing Nights for

"The Lizard of Ahhs." In all, I saw all four performances and continued this streak through every production of two high school plays she wrote and a handful more in college and beyond.

Now my daughter was giving a reading of one of her published short stories at San Jose State's Center for Steinbeck Studies and my proud run was about to end.

I had attended her first reading as a Steinbeck Fellow six months earlier, but this time my wife would be on hand (and also visiting her mother in the Bay Area for a milestone birthday) while I stayed home, dog-sitting as our boxer Murray does not fare well in the kennel.

I rationalized to Scott that I was just thankful to have not missed any big events when my daughter was young because, after all, it mattered more then.

"It also matters when they are grown," Scott replied, wisely. After a brief pause he added a command: "You *must* go."

Robert Louis Stevenson was not always right when he wrote, "To travel hopefully is a better thing than to arrive." Arriving the next evening was a far better thing than hopefully anticipating my daughter's surprised delight during my three hundred and thirty-mile drive.

As expected, she teared up instantly when she caught a glimpse of me—and I did likewise during her reading of an emotional story. Indeed, the eleven hours of

31

travel sandwiched around a much-too-brief three-hour visit was beyond worth it. As Mark Twain observed, "To get the full value of joy you must have somebody to share it with."

I had to share it with her in person.

I encourage you to similarly heed Scott's sagacity with your own children, be they young or any age. But, as my friend believes, does it truly matter as much when they are grown?

Here's my answer: "Daddy, I'll remember this for the rest of my life," my daughter whispered in my ear during our goodbye hug.

But even that sweetness was not the evening's pinnacle for me. Trumping that is how when my daughter saw me walk into the room, she says she was not really surprised.

Eight

Requiem for the Typewriter

——

MARK Twain's celebrated witticism, "The reports of my death are greatly exaggerated," came to mind the other day when another famous death was reported, and exaggerated, if only slightly.

The typewriter.

According to a newspaper story in India's *Business Standard*, Godrej & Boyce Manufacturing Co. in Mumbai has stopped production and is selling off its final five hundred typewriters.

However, obituaries headlined "The World's Last Typewriter Factory Closes In India" were premature. It turns out Godrej & Boyce was the last known producer of *manual* typewriters; a few companies remain that manufacture electric typewriters—albeit in small numbers for an ever-shrinking population of old-school dinosaurs.

Borrowing Twain's quip seems apropos considering he was an early adopter of the first practical modern typewriter patented by Christopher Latham Sholes in 1868 and manufactured by Remington Arms Company. Indeed, Twain is believed to be the first author to submit a typewritten manuscript—*Life on the Mississippi*—to a publisher.

In the *Business Standard* story, Milind Dukle of Godrej & Boyce noted the company produced only 10,000 to 12,000 office typewriters annually for the past decade. And what has become of the factory now? It has been converted to manufacture refrigerators.

The cold truth is that typewriters have been an endangered species for decades.

It is also true that like many others of my ilk, typewriters are dear to my heart. I am of the last generation of journalists who actually worked in newsrooms with manual typewriters; at UC Santa Barbara's *Daily Nexus* that is all we had. And in my first newspaper job after college in 1982 with the Twentynine Palms *Desert Trail*, the office boasted but a single newfangled word processor with a floppy disk; hence writers composed their stories on manual typewriters and then took turns retyping them into the lone computer in order to be electronically typeset.

By the time I arrived at *The Ventura County Star*—nee *Star-Free Press*—in 1987, computers had taken over the newsroom although I recall that the legendary Julius Gius banged out his wonderful weekly "Editor's Notebook" and post-retirement guest essays on a manual typewriter until his death in 1996. Similarly, the late, great local columnist Chuck Thomas long favored his trusty Remington typewriter because it never crashed and lost what he had just written. "Computers," he would lament, "are supposed to make life easier not more difficult."

Yes, to my ears the rhythmic *rat-a-tat-tat* of fingers pounding manual typewriter keys and the *"Ding! ... Ding! ... Ding!"* of tab bells ringing and then the *"Zippity-clank! ... Zippity-clank!"* of return carriages being flung back to begin a new line created a lovely newsroom symphony. Not that I would actually want to go back to the days of messy ink ribbons, type-bars that jammed, and copyediting with a pencil and symbols instead of a delete key or electronically moving blocks of copy.

With that said, I actually do on rare occasion type notes and letters on a manual typewriter—a classic Underwood No. 5 (circa 1920) that had belonged to my paternal grandfather. It is the same model favored by, among many great others, F. Scott Fitzgerald, Carl Sandburg, James Thurber, and Thornton W. Burgess (whose mint-condition antique is on display in his museum in East Sandwich, Massachusetts, and gave me a thrill to see). Grandpa Ansel's No. 5 had fallen into disrepair when I inherited it so I spent six months painstakingly cleaning it inside and out, from A to Z and 0 to 9, bringing it into sparkling condition.

Getting it into working condition, however, posed two final hurdles: by the early 1980s, it was difficult to find an ink ribbon for it and next-to-impossible to locate a Q key to replace the one that was missing. After learning that Andy Rooney collected Underwood No. 5s so he would have spare parts to repair his own favored machine, I took a wild shot in the dark and wrote him about my predicament. Remarkably, and kindly, he mailed me a replacement Q key.

The keys that come to mind today, however, are I, P and R

R.I.P. the manual typewriter: 1868-2011.

I, of course, composed this essay on a computer not a typewriter—yet I did type it on a keyboard just like Mark Twain used for his *Life on the Mississippi* manuscript. Indeed, so long as there are personal computers—and smart phones and tablets—long live QWERTY.

Nine

Beautiful Imperfection

———

"HOW long does it take you to write a column?"

It is a question I am often asked when speaking to a classroom of kids or a service group of adults or a book club. I really have no good answer other than, "About twice as long as it should because I am a painfully slow writer—but usually not long enough because my deadline seems to arrive before I am completely satisfied."

This is as true now with a week to write a column as it was in the press box with as little as ten minutes to file from game's end to deadline. Indeed, I have found truth in Leonardo da Vinci's observation: "Art is never finished, only abandoned."

And yet historians suggest da Vinci had a difficult time abandoning his art fully, as it is believed he worked on the Mona Lisa, off and on, for possibly sixteen years, including twelve years on the lips.

Thank goodness for deadlines that force a writer to abandon his or her art. Indeed, a deadline is penicillin for the bacteria *writer's blockitis* and a miracle salve for the ailment *paralysis by perfectionism*.

"Perfectionism is the enemy of creation, as extreme self-solitude is the enemy of well-being," said the prolific writer John Updike.

Volitare was more succinct, noting: "The perfect is the enemy of the good."

Nonetheless, I still believe that in writing—as in most endeavors—time and effort are allies of the good becoming better. Certainly I think a column I spend many hours on, and rewrite and polish and rewrite and polish some more, will rise above one I bang out in a couple hours.

"Aim at perfection in everything, though in most things it is unattainable," advised Lord Chesterfield. "However, they who aim at it, and persevere, will come much nearer to it than those whose laziness and despondency make them give it up as unattainable."
John Wooden put it similarly: "Perfection is an impossibility, but striving for perfection is not. Do the best you can. That is what counts."

I recently learned that the Shakers, renowned for their furniture design and craftsmanship, had their own vaccine for Type-A perfectionism—they deliberately introduced a "mistake" into the things they made in order to show that man should not aspire to the perfection of

God. Flawed, they believed, could be ideal.

Perhaps many of us can take a lesson here from the Shakers. Maybe we don't figuratively need a gold star and "Perfect" written in red ink at the top of the page of everything we undertake. Maybe, instead, we need to be proud of doing our best; of making an effort that counts. Maybe we need to see our creativity, not negativity, when we draw outside the lines. Maybe we need to embrace the effort, not the finishing clock, when we don't set a new PR in a 5K or marathon.

Maybe we need to ignore advertising that makes us believe that only a wrinkle-free, gray-free, pimples-free, fill-in-the-blank-free appearance is beauty perfection.

Similar to the Shakers, the Navajos purposely weave a single imperfection into their handmade patterned blankets. To their eyes this makes the blankets more, not less, beautiful.

In his terrific book, *Blood and Thunder: The Epic Story of Kit Carson and the Conquest of the American West*, author Hampton Sides elaborates on this mindset:

"Navajos hated to complete anything—whether it was a basket, a blanket, a song, or a story. They never wanted their artifacts to be too perfect, or too close-ended, for a definitive ending cramped the spirit of the creator and sapped the life from the art. So they left little gaps and imperfections, deliberate lacunae that kept things alive for another day.

"Even today Navajo blankets often have a faint imperfection designed to let the creation breathe—a thin line that originates from the center and extends all the way to the edge, sometimes with a single thread dangling from its border. Tellingly, the Navajos call the intentional flaw the 'spirit outlet.' "

Henceforth, I will keep the Shakers and Navajos in mind with my writing—and other undertakings—and embrace imperfections. However, I will not intentionally weave a mistake into my essays, as I am confident my "spirit outlet" will occur on its own.

Ten

Hollywood Tale

———

THE other day a friend asked if I had ever considered writing a movie script. To my credit, I didn't end our friendship on the spot.

Let me explain. I once gave it a whirl and like most screenwriters—wannabe greenhorns to green-lighted veterans alike—I ended up secretly wishing revenge on a movie producer who has lied through white-capped teeth.

Binding the snake's hands, putting a pillowcase over his head, cracking a rib and basically scaring the living daylights out of him during a nighttime home break-in admittedly might be a tad extreme.

Depending on your definition of "tad."

My Hollywood tale began in Lana Turner-like fashion. Instead of being "discovered" on a stool at the soda fountain in Schwab's Pharmacy on Sunset Boulevard, I was at my desk in *The Star* newsroom. A reader phoned the sports desk, requested to speak to me, said he admired my columns, and asked if I would be interested in writing a screenplay for him.

I reacted the way my wife did one evening when Los Angeles Dodgers famed broadcaster Vin Scully returned my phone call at home: she thought it was a friend playing a practical joke and hung up. Like Mr. Golden Voice, Mr. Silver Screen Movie Producer called right back. He insisted he was serious. I insisted I was not interested. He persisted. I agreed to meet him.

Mr. Movie Producer's home (pronounced "mansion") at the top of a long, winding driveway in a Shangri-la neighborhood took my breath away. When he opened the ten-foot-tall elaborately carved art piece of a front door he "had me at hello."

By the time I said goodbye two hours later, Mr. Movie Producer had shown me a rough edit of a film he was wrapping up (I actually recognized a few of the actors) and we had hashed out some ideas for a *Remember The Titans*-like plot I would write. I should mention this was a few years before *Titans* became a blockbuster. It was all so serendipitous.

There were, however, a few wrinkles in the red carpet to trip over: I had never written a screenplay; never taken a screenwriting class; did not even know how to properly format the text of a script.

"No problem, no worries, no big deal! Writing a sports column is harder," Mr. Movie Producer insisted.

"Introduce all the characters in the first five pages, give the plot a twist at page thirty and another at page sixty," he explained.

"Buy a screenwriting program and a new laptop and I'll pay you back," he promised.

I delivered a script that Mr. Movie Producer insisted he loved; he delivered excuses and delays, but never a nickel reimbursement for the screenwriting software, much less a dime of the $5,000 writing fee for a first draft he guaranteed.

In truth, I was not ten percent so gullible as to think there wasn't a ninety percent likelihood I would get stiffed; I saw it as motivation to write a screenplay and an excuse to get a new laptop computer.

Still, I would be lying if I did not admit to dreaming of movie success and becoming nicknamed "Hollywoody." So when Mr. Movie Producer stopped phoning me and started ignoring my calls, I was a little peeved.

While I gave up big-screen hopes for my script— working title, "Blindsided" (long before *The Blind Side* became a box-office hit)—I held on to wishing I would one day come across *my movie* as a straight-to-DVD release and I could, in true Hollywood fashion, blindside Mr. Movie Producer with a lawsuit.

Fast forward a number of years when I read a

newspaper story about a late-night home invasion by two masked gunmen. They reportedly tied up the homeowner, who had been watching TV, covered his head with a pillowcase, punched him in the face and broke one of his ribs before escaping with $2,000 and some computer equipment.

When I read the victim's name I did a double take —it was Mr. Movie Producer! On the silver screen, I would have been an obvious suspect.

Indeed, I felt as lucky to have the airtight alibi— being seated in a press-box chair at a Lakers game the night it happened—as Lana Turner must have felt sitting on that famous stool at Schwab's.

Eleven

Kissing the Blarney Stone

———

PHILIP Dormer Stanhope, 4th Earl of Chesterfield in the 18th Century, famously observed: "Sex—the pleasure is momentary, the position ridiculous, and the expense damnable."

The Earl's kiss-and-tell quote could well have been about the Blarney Stone.

To be sure, the expense of traveling from Ventura County to County Cork, Ireland, where Blarney Castle is located, was damnable.

As for the position required to plant my lips on the legendary Blarney Stone, it was ridiculous indeed. Here I was atop the five-story castle built in 1446, lying supine with my head and shoulders precariously extended over a two-foot gap between the battlement floor and the outside stone wall with a ninety-foot straight drop to the earth below.

Fortunately, three steel rails have been installed to prevent a fatal fall—which happened on occasion in centuries past—but it is nonetheless unnerving to arch backwards over the parapet's edge until one's head is upside-down and facing outward in order to kiss a germ-infested block of limestone imbedded in the opposite wall below floor level.

Spider-Man would feel a twinge of acrophobia.

While risk to life and limb has been eliminated, there remains danger of a bumped forehead or scraped nose during the contortions. I earned both red badges of courage.

The acrobatic challenge actually begins with a steep climb up a claustrophobically narrow and low-ceilinged spiral maze of a staircase to reach the castle's summit.

Sir Winston Churchill is reported to have been tall to the challenge, kissing the Blarney Stone in 1912. Hollywood's Oliver Hardy, who comically starred with Stan Laurel, is also among the long list of celebrities and dignitaries said to have accomplished the feat.

Both figures famously fortify the lore of the Blarney Stone's magical power of endowing the gift of eloquence to all who kiss it, for Hardy successfully made the transition from silent movies to talkies and Churchill became arguably the greatest orator of the 20th Century.

Even beyond its celebrated rock of ages, Blarney Castle is magnificent. However, on the drive back to the hotel our cab driver insisted my wife and I find time to visit

Bunratty Castle, located one hundred kilometers north in Limerick, claiming it to be "one-hundred times more brilliant."

This sounded like a bunch of blarney.

It proved true.

Bunratty Castle is monstrous outside and gorgeous within, an architectural masterpiece of stonework rising from a riverbank into the clouds. With a drawbridge at the front entrance and imposing sentry towers at each of the four corners, it looks exactly as one thinks a medieval castle should.

Descending a twisting stairwell after enjoying a panoramic view from Bunratty's crest, I encountered a woman in ascent.

"How much further up," she asked, short of breath but full of excitement, "until we can kiss the Blarney Stone?"

Having bussed the Blarney Stone two days previous, I now possessed such gift of eloquence as to not laugh out loud at her muddle. Instead, I gently explained this was *Bunratty* Castle and unfortunately the *Blarney* Stone was in the *Blarney* Castle about sixty miles away in Cork townland.

The woman was visibly crestfallen. And embarrassed, for she shared she was a Limerick resident and had brought her visiting cousin here specifically to kiss the Blarney Stone. It would be like my taking a visitor to Southern California who dreams of riding Disneyland's iconic Matterhorn instead to Magic Mountain and getting in line for the Revolution rollercoaster.

For a different reason Irish playwright George Bernard Shaw did not kiss the Blarney Stone, passing on the opportunity because he said: "Eloquence I have enough and an overabundance."

Unlike the great Mr. Shaw, an under-abundance have I. And so my hope is the legend is true and some eloquence rubbed off on my lips, and my scraped nose, and can be transferred to my typing fingertips.

If so, the position will have been ridiculous and the expense damnable, but my pleasure from kissing the Blarney Stone far from momentary.

Twelve

Paths Less Traveled By

———

A dear friend of mine, a travel writer who has visited the four corners of the globe, always offers this reminder before I embark on a trip:

"Be sure to turn down a hidden alleyway or go inside a quiet doorway off the beaten path because that is where you will find some of the most memorable experiences."

During my recent fortnight in Ireland I again heeded Ken McAlpine's wisdom, which nicely echoes the closing lines from Robert Frost's classic poem "The Road Not Taken":

> *Two roads diverged in a wood, and I—*
> *I took the one less traveled by,*
> *And that has made all the difference.*

Hence, in addition to visiting the breathtaking Cliffs of Moher, historic Kilmainham Gaol prison and, of course, the famous Guinness Brewery at St. James Gate in Dublin, I also diverged off our planned path—and that made all the difference in discovering some not-in-a-tour-guide-book memorable experiences.

For example, during a scenic tour of County Cork, our bus stopped at Emmet Square where we were greeted by a seven-foot statue of Clonakilty's favorite son, Michael Collins. After learning about the founding father of the national self-determination movement who was assassinated in 1922, my wife and I went off to explore the town.

In an alleyway off the main street I came upon a small music shop. Inside, at the back, in a corner, was a half-hidden stairway. I went up the fourteen steps to explore. Instead of more handsome acoustic guitars and beautiful African drums, I found myself face to face with a mesmerizing oversized mask sculpture resembling Abraham Lincoln.

A second face was below Abe's copper countenance—storeowner Mark Holland, who looked up from his bookkeeping and shared: "I love it, too. Every time I look at it I see it differently and draw a new feeling from it."

Over the next half hour, while my wife wondered where I had wandered off, I learned that the artist who created the mask—its subject was anonymous, by the way, not of Lincoln—was Mark's brother, Kevin.

For good reason the mask carried a price tag of 2,500 Euro (about $3,200—proving, once again, if you have to ask you cannot afford it) because Kevin is somewhat famous. His numerous public commissioned pieces throughout Ireland include none other than the towering statue of Michael Collins in Emmet Square.

A serendipitous secret I collected upstairs off the beaten path: Collin's shoes were cast from a pair belonging to Mark and Kevin's father.

As my own shoes carried me down a road less traveled by in Galway Eire, I happened upon a much lesser-known artist—an artisan who works with rock instead of heavy metal. Michael Daif is a master stoneworker by trade; he proudly told me his stone fences and walls will still be standing a century after he dies.

Frost, whose memorable poems include "The Mending Wall" with the famous line "Good fences make good neighbors," would surely have admired Daif's skill.

In his spare time, Daif turns discarded shale shingles into engraved elegance.

For one-hundredth the price of Kevin Holland's copper mask, I brought home a lovely image of a Gaelic harp, Ireland's national symbol. Daif skillfully added his name and a personalized inscription on the back of the stone art piece as I watched.

A different signature, this one in blue ink, came

about when my wife and I walked past a small independent bookstore in Dublin one evening. Hearing laughter, we turned around, went inside and followed the voices upstairs. Staircases, it seems, can be as rich with unexpected experiences as are hidden alleyways and doorways.

And so it was Lisa and I met Irish author Caroline Finnerty, whose book launch party was wrapping up. After a pleasant conversation, she signed a copy of her new novel *Into the Night Sky* as a gift for our daughter.

Under a sunny afternoon sky in Limerick, a bronze bust caught my eye through a closed wrought iron gate off the beaten path on narrow Hartstong Street in the Georgian Quarter.

On closer inspection, the base below the familiar face read "Frank McCourt 1930-2009" with a feather quill engraved below.

By chance, and by taking a new walking route, we had stumbled upon the Frank McCourt Museum—formerly Leamy School, where young Frank attended and lived in the 1930's—honoring the Pulitzer Prize-winning author of *Angela's Ashes*.

Galway Greyhound Stadium was museum-like quiet and seemingly closed the evening we strolled past. Hoping to sneak a peak through a side gate, we found it ajar. Slipping inside rewarded us with the sight of a lone trainer working out a handful of greyhounds.

Witnessing these magnificent animals bounding forty miles per hour as if on winged paws around the quarter-mile oval in an empty stadium, at brilliant sunset, was art and poetry and another most memorable experience.

Thanks, Ken.

Thirteen

Splendid People

———

IN the southern Irish town of Clonakilty, a plaque below a statue of famed patriot Michael Collins bears the final entry in his diary from August 21, 1922, the day before he was assassinated: "The People Are Splendid."

During my wife's and my recent fortnight in Ireland those words proved emblematic. The people we met were splendid, indeed.

And, *in deed*, splendid from journey's start to finish. Wheeling our suitcases in downtown Dublin the night we arrived, we got lost looking for our hotel. Struggling with a map and double-checking street signs, we must have looked pitifully confused, even for tourists.

Suddenly four people jaywalked over to ask if we needed help. Instead of offering directions, they went out of their way to walk us to the hotel. A similar kindness later happened when we arrived in Limerick.

Yes, time and again the Irish made even famously amiable American Midwesterners seem grouchy by comparison.

At St. James's Gate Guinness Brewery, Jenny, a lovely young woman whose accent was as thick as she was thin, took a full ten minutes to ring us up in the gift shop because she was so busy conversing. Learning we were headed to County Cork, her hometown and the land of my distant family roots, she told us about a hidden gem of a café—and drew a map—where we "must" have an authentic Irish breakfast. We, of course, did.

In Cork City, the taxi ride from the train station to our hotel proved unforgettable—not just because our driver spoke even faster than he drove, but because he turned down a tip. I insisted; again he stone-cold refused, saying warmly: "You paid me fairly. Have a brilliant time!"

Another brilliant example of Irish kindness occurred during a tour of Old Galway City in an open-top double-decker bus. At a stop midway out, two middle-aged women stepped on, thinking it was a public bus. Told it was not, they asked where they could catch one because their friend was waiting for them at the city square.

"I'll take you," the bus driver cheerfully responded and refused to accept any fare.

On the drive to breathtaking Bunratty Castle our cabbie, Patrick Murphy—who was as perfectly Irish as his name suggests—patiently explained the native sport hurling. He also told me, with a wink to my wife, of a favorite pub nearby the castle where I could have "an affair with a tall, dark blonde in a gold dress" while waiting for a return taxi.

This, he noted, is how locals order a Guinness in reference to the legendary stout's ebony color and light head served in a trademark pint glass with a gold-leaf harp logo.

Over and again, we found that even more important than the places you visit are the people you meet. And not just the locals.

Our final night, Lisa and I went to a pub—after all, when in Rome—for dinner and surprisingly saw a familiar face. Seated alone was a man who had been on our Cliffs of Moher bus tour several days prior. We invited him over to join us.

What a memorable ending to an unforgettable trip the evening became.

A French Canadian from Quebec, Jasan was originally a forestry engineer before switching careers a few years ago at age sixty to become a suicide prevention counselor and university professor on the subject.

The seeds for this fascinating life path detour were planted decades earlier.

About thirty years ago, when a temporary home was needed for an abandoned infant from Senegal in West Africa, Jasan, who is white and has never married, opened his home. Too, he opened his heart and soon legally adopted the boy.

Five years later, Jasan adopted not one more child in need, but eight ten- and eleven-year-old refugee girls from Vietnam. The fact that three of his new daughters had relatives who had committed suicide eventually led Jasan into his new career.

"It makes me happy to help others," Jasan, now a grandfather more than a dozen times over, shared.

Michael Collins was right: People are splendid.

Fourteen

Welcome Home

———

IN 1792, at age fourteen—while claiming to be eighteen in order to board a ship bound for America—James Dallas sailed out of Ireland's Cork Harbor seeking a new life, likely never again to see his Old World loved ones.

Nearly two and a quarter centuries later, I marvel at my great-great-great-grandfather's hardihood.

James Dallas is the earliest documented branch of my family tree. Visiting his homeland has long beckoned me, surely as a mysterious force of nature calls an adult salmon from the ocean back to the gravel riverbeds far upstream from which it originally came.

My roots grow deep in the fertile soil near Ohio's Mad River where James Dallas settled. The next four generations, beginning with my great-great-grandfather John Woodburn (who married James Dallas' daughter), remained in Urbana and nearby Columbus until my dad moved our family to Ventura, California, four decades ago.

Heritage is dear to me: my son's middle name is

Ansel, in honor of his paternal great-grandfather; my daughter's first name is Dallas. Thus, my summer fortnight in Ireland, and especially five days spent in ancestral County Cork, promised to be a trip for the ages.

Flying twelve hours to London and two more to Dublin, before taking a three-hour train ride to Cork, seemed an arduous journey. Yet I could not help think how embarrassingly easy this was compared to weeks at sea in an 18th Century ship.

In a movie, I would have arrived in Cork and taken a taxi to a farmhouse, knocked on the front door and been greeted with open arms by a distant blood relative. Real life, of course, is rarely so Hollywood.

For starters, where would I possibly knock? I had no idea and found no new clues.

When asked about the surname "Dallas," tour guides, locals and even a historian in the Cork City Central Library did not recognize it as Irish. It was suggested the Gaelic name "*Dalgash*" might have been anglicized upon arrival to the New World.

On a nine-hour bus tour of bucolic southern Cork, our guide/professor Dan O'Brien spent an hour expounding on dairy farming. It was an invaluable lecture. Importantly, I learned that dairy farming was "the jewel of the crown" in Cork in the 1700s and 1800s. In fact, Port of Cork was the world's leading exporter of butter. So it makes perfect sense James Dallas was a dairy farmer. Indeed, he and the next two generations of my family owned a dairy farm in Ohio.

Making sense of why he left Ireland may be answered by the question in this lyric from an old Irish folk song: "Was it poverty or the call of adventure?"

Likely, both. Three decades of economic difficulty across Ireland preceded James Dallas' emigration. Add to this a system of powerful landlords and hardscrabble tenant farmers, and perhaps as much as fleeing hardship James Dallas was pursuing adventure in America and the opportunity of land ownership.

Gazing out the tour bus window at farm after farm, cow after cow, mile after mile, I wondered if against all odds I was at one of these moments looking at James Dallas' boyhood pasture. As Hemingway wrote in *The Sun Also Rises*: "Isn't it pretty to think so?"

Two more pretty thoughts: strolling through historic English Market in Cork City it came easy to imagine James Dallas once shopping here; visiting Guinness Brewery, established in 1759, I could not help but picture my forebearer, even at age fourteen, drinking a pint of the legendary black stout.

I actually had never before had a Guinness, yet at first taste at St. James Gate loved it like a newborn does mother's milk almost, as if this penchant for a pint of the "good stuff" were somehow ingrained deep in my Irish DNA nearly two centuries ago.

One more prettiness: Hearing Irish accents and pronunciations, like the silent "h" in "th"—*tirty, tousand, tirsty*—I wondered if James Dallas had carried the lilt of a leprechaun.

Prior to arriving in Ireland, James Dallas, born 182 years before I was, had seemed less a real person and more a painting faded a *tousand* years. But in the context of this ancient land where farmhouses are routinely a century old or more; stone fences built masterfully without mortar stand three hundred years later; and castles date back half a millennium, time collapsed and I suddenly felt a closer connection.

Spiritually, I felt his presence.

The day I arrived in Cork a small sign above a house doorway caught my eye—and heart: "Welcome Home." It brought to mind a poetic thought by Maya Angelou: "When you leave home, you take home with you."

Traveling to Ireland, I felt this true. Returning to America, I felt it equally.

Fifteen

Maya: "Voice of God"

—

"WHAT'S your favorite book you have ever read?" is nearly impossible to answer. One's honest response may change if asked again tomorrow or even simply an hour later.

And yet if you alter the question ever so slightly —"What is your favorite book you have ever *listened* to?"— I can answer with certainty and sincerity and consistency: *I Know Why The Caged Bird Sings* on audio book narrated by its author, Maya Angelou.

On the written page, this memoir is a modern classic. Read aloud by Angelou, it is ageless poetry.

Decades ago, James Facenda gained fame as the bass narrator of NFL Films and earned the nickname "The Voice of God." With apologies to the late Facenda, Maya Angelou made you believe god is a *She.*

The great writer and poet and humanitarian, who passed away on May 28, 2014 at age eighty-six, could have read a phonebook aloud and made it enthralling. Or the nutritional facts on a cereal box. Yes, hers was "The Voice of God."

Too, Angelou seemed to have Her wisdom and grace.

I saw Angelou perform—indeed, she did not give a lecture, she gave an intimate performance—in person only once, at the Pasadena Civic Auditorium. It was a number of years ago, but I vividly remember her sitting regally in an overstuffed chair on stage and magically making it seem like she was having a one-on-one visit with each of the three thousand-plus people in attendance.

Remarkably, Maya's great friend Tavis Smiley would later share with me his experience seeing her in the green room beforehand, breathing from an oxygen tank to build her strength just prior to going onstage.

In essence, this woman warrior was our elegant host for the evening, and yet one of the stories she shared that has most clearly stayed with me was about the importance of being a gracious guest.

I forget precisely what impoverished village she was visiting in a distant land, in Africa I believe, but her hosts served a fancy porridge for dinner. Upon taking her first spoonful, Angelou realized the "raisins" were alive.

The second impulse in such a situation—the first being to gag—is to spit out the wriggling intruders. Angelou did a third thing, an amazing and rare thing: she swallowed that unappetizing mouthful—and, more remarkably and more thoughtfully, she smiled and kept eating spoonful after spoonful until it was all gone.

You see, Angelou realized she had been given an honorary meal that her hosts considered a delicacy. To decline, even politely, would be an insult. And so Maya Angelou, who would rather fall ill than be ill-thought-of as rude, behaved as if she were dining on her favorite five-star cuisine.

I have thought of this life lesson from Angelou over the years when hearing people complain to a hostess that they can't eat this or won't eat that or the other. I mean, if Angelou could affably eat some squirming "raisins" perhaps those of us who are particular about what we do— and don't—eat could (unless we have a true allergy or medical restriction) politely tolerate a smidgen of dairy, gluten, sugar or whatever.

And yet, the opposite also holds true: I believe Angelou would have gracefully wanted to provide a gluten-free, lactose-free or a vegetarian dish to any of her guests who desired one. To be sure, one gets the feeling Angelou lived the words she preached, such as:

"Try to be a rainbow in someone's cloud."

"If you don't like something, change it. If you can't change it, change your attitude."

"When you leave home, you take home with you."

"As long as you're breathing, it's never too late to do some good."

"You can only become truly accomplished at something you love. Don't make money your goal. Instead pursue the things you love doing."

"A friend may be waiting behind a stranger's face."

"Love recognizes no barriers. It jumps hurdles, leaps fences, penetrates walls to arrive at its destination full of hope."

"When you learn, teach; when you get, give."

And: "I've learned that people will forget what you said, people will forget what you did, but people will never forget how you made them feel."

Somewhere, in some distant land, there are people who feel like Maya Angelou loved the authentic local delicacy meal of honor they served her. Actually, all around the globe there are people who remember feeling her rare grace.

Indeed, the quote from Maya Angelou that seems most fitting in the wake of her passing are the words she said upon Nelson Mandela's death: "Our planet has lost a friend."

Sixteen

Two Special Hoosiers

———

TWENTY-SEVEN years ago this month (March 30, 2014), half my lifetime ago, I received the most wonderful of invitations when John Wooden asked me to join him for a four-mile morning walk.

This week I received another heady invite—to be a guest on "The Tavis Smiley Show" to reminisce about Coach Wooden.

Airing on Public Radio International, the show reaches more than seven hundred affiliates nationwide. For an author, it is a momentous opportunity. But to be honest, it would have mattered little to me if the mic had failed to record the interview.

No, the thrill among thrills was getting to meet Smiley, whom I have long admired for his gifts as TV and radio host, publisher and best-selling author—and above all for his life-changing philanthropic work. At age forty-nine, Smiley has accomplished enough for three lifetimes. He must get by on two hours sleep.

Though four years my junior, Smiley has been a hero I look up to.

The risk with meeting heroes in person is they rarely measure up to the ideals in your mind. Smiley, however, did not disappoint. Rather, he exceeded all expectations. In this manner and more, Tavis Smiley reminds me greatly of John Wooden, my all-time idol. This is the highest of compliments I can give; one I rarely have; and it is also fully merited here.

The similarities begin with both having grown up in Indiana and working their way through college: Wooden at Purdue and Smiley at rival Indiana University after arriving on campus with a mere fifty dollars in his pocket.

It comes as no surprise when Smiley says the two Hoosiers hit it off swimmingly from their first hello when they met for an interview a number of years ago.

Why wouldn't they? Smiley epitomizes all fifteen blocks in Wooden's famous Pyramid of Success—Industriousness, Friendship, Loyalty, Cooperation, Enthusiasm, Self-Control, Alertness, Initiative, Intentness, Condition, Skill, Team Spirit, Poise, Confidence, and Competitive Greatness.

As a specific example, consider "Intentness" which Wooden defined thusly: "Stay the course. When thwarted try again; harder; smarter. Persevere relentlessly."

As a college junior, Smiley wrote a letter each week,

month after month after month, to Los Angeles Mayor Tom Bradley seeking a summer internship.

Thwarted, Smiley bought an airline ticket he could ill afford and flew to L.A.—without an appointment—to try to achieve his goal through a personal appeal.

Again told there were no internships available, Smiley persevered. He sent a handwritten letter "from the heart" to Bradley and finally received a coveted position.

Smiley has used this same Competitive Greatness to win his own Wooden-like collection of NCAA basketball titles, so to speak, including being named one of "The World's 100 Most Influential People" by *TIME* magazine; receiving the prestigious Du Bois Medal from Harvard University; and honored with a star on the Hollywood Walk of Fame.

Another similarity: Smiley's signature "Keep the faith" TV sign-off always makes me think of Wooden because the top block of the Pyramid of Success is held in place by a special mortar comprised of two ingredients: Faith and Patience. To be sure, these two devout Hoosiers are cut from the same rare cloth.

"Things turn out best for those who make the best of the way things turn out," Wooden liked to say, while Smiley frequently quotes his grandmother's advice, "There is a lesson, and a blessing, in everything we go through."

Another "Wooden-ism" embodied by Smiley: "You

can't live a perfect day without doing something for someone who will never be able to repay you." He does so through numerous philanthropic donations and deeds, including his nonprofit foundation that has provided "Youth to Leaders" training workshops and conferences to more than six thousand youngsters.

Indeed, Smiley shares Wooden's belief that "young people need fewer critics and more models."

This is actually true for people of all ages.

Before I left the Sheryl Flowers Radio Studios in Los Angeles, Smiley was expressing his admiration for Coach Wooden and Muhammad Ali, among other heroes of his, and opined: "We don't make 'em like that anymore."

"Sure we do," I countered. "Look in the mirror."

Tavis Smiley smiled modestly, said thanks sincerely, but disagreed humbly.

It is exactly how John Wooden used to respond to superlative praise, no matter how rightly deserved.

———

Postscript: Just as my first interview of Coach John Wooden was soon followed by an invitation to join him for a morning walk and breakfast, and from there a friendship grew, so did my interview by Tavis Smiley lead to a lunch—and my first sampling of delicious Caribbean cuisine!—and a new friendship.

Seventeen

Greggie and "The Greatest"

——

IN more than twenty-five years as a sports columnist, I met and interviewed a "Who's Who" of greats, including "The Greatest" himself, Muhammad Ali.

My greatest memory of The Greatest happened shortly before Ali lit the Olympic flame at the opening ceremonies of the 1996 Summer Olympics in Atlanta.

The living legend shuffled into the room at an autograph show in the cavernous Anaheim Convention Center, his feet sliding forward slowly and carefully in the unsteady gait of an old man missing his cane.

Ali was only fifty-four years old that day. Fifty-four going on ninety-four, it seemed. Parkinson's Syndrome has caused a new "Ali Shuffle."

Still, he remained indisputably the people's champion. When the doors for the National Sports Collectors Convention opened two hours before his noon appearance, fans rushed to get into a line that swelled to three hundred by The Champ's arrival. Meanwhile, Hall-of-Fame baseball and football players sat nearby, lonely almost, with Sharpie pens capped.

Ali's hands never got a rest, never stopped moving, even when he wasn't signing endless autographs. His hands shook so uncontrollably it looked like he was constantly shuffling a deck of cards. The invisible "Ali Shuffle."

And yet once he began signing the cursive "M" until he had dotted the lower-case "i", the earthquake in Ali's hands magically calmed. Indeed, his signature was smooth and true. Perhaps after signing his name a million times, his neurons and synapses are programmed with a computer-like save-get keystroke.

But Ali was no robotic signing machine. He smiled whenever, which was almost always, an autograph seeker paying $90 to have a flat item signed—and a whopping $120 on a boxing glove—called him "Champ" or said "It's an honor to meet you."

A steep price for a squiggle of ink? Not at all when you consider one man in line called it "a religious experience."

And every time a camera was raised, Ali, his face still "pretty" and his body still muscular and almost in fighting trim in a tan golf shirt, would rise out of his chair, slowly but gracefully and without assistance, to pose with a clenched fist held beneath the fan's chin.

When I had learned Muhammad Ali would be in town, I made plans to take my then-six-year-old son Greggie to see him, just as my grandfather once took my dad to see the larger-than-life Babe Ruth in a hotel lobby.

All day beforehand I had schooled the little boy about Ali, telling him again and again how he is "The Greatest."

With the handy excuse of me working on a column for the next morning's newspaper, we hung out right beside The Champ for half an hour as he signed glossy pictures and signed magazine covers and signed boxing gloves. Finally, I told my son it was time to leave.

He disagreed.

"Not yet. I've gotta say 'Hi,' " he whispered, and loudly.

Ali heard the little boy's protests. The great man turned around and instinctively the little boy stepped forward and extended his right hand. Ali, who had shaken adult hands almost femininely with just his manicured fingertips, took the small hand gently into his big paw and this time it did not look awkward or weak or sad.

And, for the very first time in thirty minutes, the man who used to "float like a butterfly" broke out of his cocoon of total silence.

"Hi, Little Man," Ali whispered, spreading his arms wide open.

The six-year-old Little Man, who back then was quite shy, instantly stepped forward and was wrapped in a clinch. Goodness it was cool.

But it turned out the real Kodak moment was yet to come.

After a standing eight count, or maybe even a full ten seconds, Ali freed the Little Man and then held his right palm out in the universal "give me five" position.

The boy, who at that age smacked hands hard enough to shatter metatarsals, *gently* slapped Al's extended palm before then holding out his own tiny palm for The Champ to return the gesture.

Ali took a swipe...

... and missed.

At the very last instant, the Little Man, as he loved to do, pulled his hand away like a matador's red cape teasing a bull.

"Too slow," the Little Man whispered, his two missing front teeth causing the words to lisp slightly. Like, *"Tooooth lowww."* Like Ali's own soft voice that now lisps slightly.

And like two six-year-olds they laughed together at the prank.

While still roaring in delight, Ali once again opened his arms and my son once again stepped into them, except this time the shy boy squeezed back, and tightly, as though he were hugging his dear Grandpa. Ali's eyes caught mine and I swear to this day they twinkled.

It was an end-of-a-movie fade-out and roll-the-credits hug. A full thirty-second hug. A worth-the-hour-and-a-half-drive-in-Southern-California-gridlocked-freeway-traffic hug.

A hug from "The Greatest" that the Little Man, now a six-foot-three-tall man, still remembers warmly, and surely will until he is an old man.

As we walked hand-in-hand away after saying goodbye to Ali, my son stopped and looked up at me and here is what he said through a Christmas-morning smile with his missing-teeth lisp: "You know, Dad, you were right—he really is The Bestest."

Eighteen

A Slant on Autographs

———

THE Black Death had a rival scourge in the Middle Ages. Call it The Black Ink, because according to historians the pursuit of autographs dates back to this period. It seems the hunt for signatures of the famous came about after the hunt for religious relics waned.

Centuries after the bubonic plague had been largely erased, Albert Einstein weighed in with his scientific view on the autograph, terming it the last vestige of cannibalism.

After three decades of watching the signature savageness as a sports columnist, including seeing grown men push children out of the way in pursuit of autographs, I think Einstein was being too kind.

But something really cool happened not long ago that changed my viewpoint. An autograph show was held in a hotel lobby in the historic town of Gettysburg and instead of home-run heroes and Hall-of-Fame slam dunkers and Olympic gold medalists, the "heroes" signing their signatures truly were heroes. Specifically, they numbered nearly half of the seventy-nine current surviving recipients of the Medal of Honor—our nation's highest military award.

If I collected inked autographs, these warriors' *John Hancocks* would be on my Most Wanted List.

Instead, over the years I have collected autographs of a different slant: oddball stories from athletes I've interviewed. Let me share a few.

"I am frequently asked to sign Pennzoil cans," shared Arnold Palmer, who has done countless TV commercials for the petroleum product.

Similarly, Hall of Fame pitcher—and Advil pitchman—Nolan Ryan said he often gets asked to autograph bottles of the pain reliever.

"I enjoy people, so I don't mind autograph requests at all," legendary Dodgers broadcaster Vin Scully began. "Why not sign? They're paying me a compliment by asking."

And what are some of the stranger "compliments" he's had?

"I've signed a lot of baseballs as you can imagine, but also golf balls and even a hockey puck which is sort of strange, I should think," Scully continued. "Paper napkins seem popular—even dirty napkins. I think it's all they have on hand. I don't expect them to keep it, but I sign anyway because hopefully they will keep the moment."

"I've signed dollar bills for homeless people who you know were going to spend it and not save it," echoed Olympic gymnastics champion Kerri Strug. "And I've signed first-graders' body parts with pencils, which is hard to do."

Skin is popular from head to toe. I've seen Magic Johnson sign a bald head with a black Sharpie marker and Muhammad Ali do so on kids' arms, legs and feet. But the most memorable thing I saw Ali autograph was the front of a jogging bra...

... still being worn by the young woman.

Speaking of dirty laundry, Olympic softball gold medalist Kim Maher added this footnote to my signature collection: "A kid handed me a sock to autograph—a gross, dirty sock!"

Did she sign it?

Maher: "Oh, yeah, of course!"

Olympic marathon champion Frank Shorter can relate: "Over the years I've been asked to sign some pretty grungy running shoes."

Echoed Billy Mills, America's last Olympic gold-medal winner in the 10,000 meters in 1964: "I was asked by a school fundraiser to send an autographed pair of shoes. 'The worse-smelling the better,' they said." He compromised by sending a pair he had worn only a couple times.

More memorable laundry. "The oddest thing I've been asked to autograph is a diaper," Carl Lewis replied, chuckling at the memory. The nine-time Olympic gold medalist went on: "Luckily it wasn't on the baby at the time —the mom pulled it out of a bag. I'd have had to draw the line at signing a dirty diaper, I think."

Fellow American Olympic sprinter Jon Drummond might have crossed that line, noting: "I was once asked to sign a baby's diaper—while the baby was wearing it."

Um, *bottom* line, did he sign?

"Yep," Drummond answered. "If they kept the autograph, I hope they changed the diaper before it was too late."

What would Einstein think?

I think a soiled napkin suddenly seems like a nice keepsake.

Nineteen

Some "Magic" Moments

———

I T was the littlest of things, yet it remains an indelible memory more than a quarter century later. A small gesture of gracefulness telling a bigger story.

I was in the Los Angeles Lakers' locker room as a rookie writer. It was after the game and reporters were boxing one another out around Magic Johnson's locker stall like power forwards and centers battling for rebound position.

As the scrum of scribes and TV cameras thinned, I moved forward and finally asked a question to which Magic prefaced his answer: "Well, Woody... "

Understand, I was not a familiar beat writer. Rather, this was my first time covering a Lakers game. But Magic had the grace to slyly spy the name on my media credential and make me feel welcomed.

Truth is, Magic made every media member feel welcomed—and made our working lives much easier.

Unlike Kareem Abdul-Jabbar, who would often

escape to the showers without talking to us, or Shaq O'Neal, who seemed to delight in mumbling so we couldn't hear what he was saying, Magic would sit at his locker and thoughtfully answer each and every question until the very last reporter had what he or she needed.

I had the good fortune to interview Magic many more times during the final few years of his playing career and also enjoyed a couple lengthy one-on-one conversations with him at his youth summer basketball camps at Cal Lutheran University in Thousand Oaks, California, after he retired. Every encounter was a pleasure.

For good reason when people ask me who my favorite person to interview has been, the first name I mention after John Wooden is Magic Johnson.

So when the basketball legend turned entrepreneur and philanthropist was a guest speaker not long ago as part of UC Santa Barbara's Arts & Lectures series at the Arlington Theatre, I had to be there.

I am glad I was. I have seen many wonderful speakers on stage—including Maya Angelou, Malcolm Gladwell, the Dalai Lama, and youngest-ever Nobel Peace Prize honoree Malala Yousafzai—and Magic is second to none.

He also did something unique—he ignored the lectern, eschewed a chair, and in fact shunned the stage entirely. Instead, in theatric terms he "broke the fourth wall" and gave his nearly two-hour-long talk from the floor in front of the stage as well as intimately walking up and down the aisles.

After recounting how he and his strapped college dorm mates at Michigan State University would clip coupons and pool their money to buy one large pizza and a few sodas to share, Magic thoughtfully walked to the back of the auditorium to address the UCSB students who suddenly went from being in the cheap seats to having a front-row view.

Along the way, the extra "charisma" nucleotide in Magic's DNA was evident as he stopped and talked, and posed for snapshots at his own request, with a handful of audience members. An hour later—reminiscent of my long-ago locker room encounter, except this time there were no name badges—Magic addressed a couple of these same strangers by first name, having made the classy effort to remember them.

Magic has treated F. Scott Fitzgerald's famous declaration, "There are no second acts in American lives," like a backpedaling defender. He faked it out and scored. Impossibly, Magic has been as successful in the business boardroom as he was fast-breaking between the backboards.

A tweet-length post-NBA summary in one hundred and forty characters: Part owner of the Los Angeles

Dodgers; owner of movie theaters, Starbucks, 24 Hour Fitness and Burger King franchises serving urban areas; philanthropist; and HIV/AIDS activist.

Directing his wisdom directly to the "young people" in the Santa Barbara audience, Magic, now fifty-five, encouraged them to pursue their education, find mentors, and dream big.

"I was a student-athlete who went to class," he shared.

"People helped me along the way so I need to help others."

"I was poor, but I didn't dream poor."

Further advice for success in the business world, and life, included: "Respect people's time"; "always be early"; and "over-deliver."

"I want you to over-deliver to everybody; your parents; your professor," Magic concluded. "That's what we all have to do now. It's not enough just to deliver anymore. You have to over-deliver."

It was not lip service: Magic was scheduled to speak for an hour and a half but graciously over-delivered by nearly thirty minutes.

Happily, Magic-ally, some things never change.

Twenty

Kings Are Royal Success

——

EACH season prior to the first tip-off, John Wooden would evaluate his team's talent, study UCLA's schedule and, after considerable thought, write on a slip of paper how many basketball games he thought his Bruins would win.

The secret prediction would be sealed inside an envelope, not to be opened until season's end. Amazingly, the Wizard of Westwood sometimes hit the win total right on the button.

A number of years ago, as coach of the sixth-grade Kings, I readied a similar envelope. Before revealing my prediction tucked inside, first a recap.

The youth league season began with a twenty-point loss and only some lucky shots where the basket somehow got in the way of the ball kept it that close.

The Kings' second game was even more deflating.

But after an 0-3 start, a funny thing happened. The Kings stopped walking without dribbling and started passing to the open man. Now and then they made two, three, even five quick passes that resulted in a layup. They switched on defense, set picks on offense. At times it was beautiful.

Beautiful, too, were their beaming smiles as they closed out the regular season with a five-game winning streak.

I have long since forgotten the specific victories, but I still remember the improvement the boys made and the sportsmanship they showed. Being good winners is easy, but the boys handled defeat with grace as well—a much greater and more rare thing. They were actually happier following a couple losses where they played quite well than after a sloppy win. They recognized, as Coach Wooden always emphasized, that a scoreboard is not always an accurate measure of success.

I remember one of the Kings' smallest players, Joseph, setting brick-wall picks.

I remember Kellen being even tougher, checking his blood sugar level between quarters and sometimes playing with a tube in his arm running to a miniature insulin pump. I wish every prima-donna pro player could have seen him play.

I remember that no one ever came to practice or games wearing a bigger smile than did Kirby, which is all the more remarkable when you know that his aunt died a few weeks into the season.

I remember how much all the boys delighted in playing the free-throw game "Thunder" and how they celebrated when one of them would knock me out.

I remember a couple of scoreless quarters; passes to nobody; dribbles that went off our own toes and out of bounds; air ball layups; and times the Kings seemed to forget every single thing we ever worked on in practice.

But I also remember those times when these young Kings looked like the NBA's Sacramento Kings. The flashes where they ran the pick-and-roll as perfectly as John Stockton and Karl Malone, and a few inbound plays executed so expertly they would have made Phil Jackson proud.

Usually, the rare basketball rainbows were gone as quickly as they appeared. Still, they were worth the vigil.

I also remember a lot of moments involving my son, none more than after Joe scored back-to-back fifteen-footers. The next trip down the court, my son passed up an open shot and made sure Joe got another look. He missed, but that wasn't the point.

The point was this: a few weeks earlier I had shared with my son that Magic Johnson once told me that if a guy made two shots in a row, *the next shot was his* even if someone else was wide open.

My son ran a play for Joe. Running back down the court he smiled at me. He had remembered the lesson.

Back, now, to the sealed envelope. I was tempted to write down "3" for the number of wins I thought we would get. It would have proven a great underestimation of these boys. They lacked height, but not fortitude, and finished with a 6-5 record.

But I did not write down "3" or any number at all. Instead, this is the prediction I wrote: "We will have fun." Did I hit it on the button? Well, after a heartbreaking loss in the playoffs where the Kings gamely rallied from ten points down to take the lead, only to ultimately fall short, I got my answer.

"Coach," one of my favorite players in eight years of coaching youth sports told me after the final buzzer, his smile defying the scoreboard, "I sure had a lot of fun this season."

So did I, Gage. So did I.

Twenty-One

"Poem" Becomes Woodchips

ONE hundred years ago Joyce Kilmer penned "Trees" with one of the most widely familiar opening couplets in America poetry:

> *I think that I shall never see / A poem lovely as a tree.*

The other morning, I looked out my window and across the street as a lovely "poem" was sawed down, cut up, turned into woodchips and trucked away.

It was like seeing a theatrical street version of Shel Silverstein's classic children's book *The Giving Tree* starring two workmen in white hardhats and optic-yellow vests.

Actually, this story was even sadder, for this tree's limbs were not used to build a house for the grown boy; its trunk not crafted into a boat to sail the seas. When the workmen's work was finished, there was not even a stump left to sit upon and rest.

An arborist could tell you what type of tree this was, but I cannot. Were I to venture a guess, unable as I was to count its rings, wise readers would surely point out my ignorance. No matter. What is important is it was majestic, perhaps seventy feet tall, and leafy with a trunk I could not reach my arms around. Indeed, it was a venerable tree worthy of hugging.

Something else important: the tree had become a botanical Leaning Tower of Pisa, cracking and raising a section of sidewalk. And if it toppled, it would fall across a busy street. Too large to be braced or straightened, the tree was a danger that surely needed to come down.

And so at 9 a.m. a whining chainsaw turned an overcast morning tenfold gloomier. Standing in the basket of a gargantuan yellow cherry-picker, a workman cut off the large branches one by one by one as he hydraulically rose higher and higher and higher.

Far below, the felled branches were cut into manageable lengths and fed into a woodchipper that roared like a jet engine. Lines of a lovely "poem" went in, ugly mulch came out.

And then the tall barren trunk came down, made not into lumber for a home or boat, but into short logs to be burned in fireplaces. This was not a heartwarming thought. From start to finish, what took decades and decades to become living poetry was eliminated in less than four hours. It was tree-mendously sad.

It was not my tree, not in my backyard, and yet it was mine and yours because trees are for all of us to enjoy.

Trees are one of nature's Hallmark cards—an ironic thought since some trees literally become greeting cards. Or, more irony here, pages in a book.

Kilmer again: *A tree that may in summer wear / A nest of robins in her hair.*

No more birds will nest in the lovely tree I used to see out my kitchen window looking east, the sun rising above "her hair" in the late spring mornings.

The melancholy event gave me pause to think about a handful of memorable trees in my life: The evergreen beside the driveway of my first boyhood home that my two older brothers and I attempted blind shots over during games of H-O-R-S-E. The sturdy buckeye nut tree near a swimming hole we swung from on a rope. The apple tree in the backyard of my first crush, Lisa Bautista, that I picked snacks from its lower branches on a shortcut home from elementary school. The orange tree my two then-young children and I planted in their very first backyard. The giant redwoods we saw, in awe, as a family. And on and on.

I think "poems" fill all our lives more than we generally realize. We draw trees in kindergarten and climb trees as older kids and hopefully at least once in our lives plant a tree, for as the Greek proverb states: "A society grows great when old men plant trees whose shade they know they shall never sit in."

Kilmer once more: *Poems are made by fools like me, / But only God can make a tree.*

Afterwards, this writer fool walked over to determine how old the tree had been by counting its rings, but the stump was cut off below the ground and covered with dirt.

I may be overestimating by half, but I like to think this tree had sprouted in 1913, the same year as "Trees" came into being.

Twenty-Two

Keep America Beautiful

——

THE wadded-up fast-food bag hit the shoulder of the road two running strides ahead of me like a wild Major League fastball in the dirt, its velocity aided by being thrown from a car traveling at least sixty miles per hour.

After my heart started up again and my silent cursing stopped, I thought of actor Iron Eyes Cody and the famous "Keep America Beautiful" television commercial he appeared in during my boyhood in the early 1970s.

The national public service ad featured a stoic Native American chief—played by Cody—whose proud face was as deeply lined as plowed field. A single lonely teardrop slowly rolled down his cheek after he saw litter being tossed out the window of a passing car.

The "Keep America Beautiful" campaign lived up to its name, reportedly reducing litter at one point by as much as eight-eight percent in three hundred communities throughout thirty-eight states.

Four decades later, I think Iron Eyes would be

openly sobbing. According to recent statistics, more than fifty-one billion pieces of litter land on American roadways annually—that is 6,729 items per mile of road! Moreover, litter's life span is staggering: it is estimated an aluminum can takes two hundred years to decompose; plastic six-pack rings, four hundred and fifty years; a glass bottle, one million years. Even a cigarette butt takes up to five years to decompose.

Here is another ugly sight I recently saw: a park bench littered with an orange peel, an empty water bottle, a dirty napkin and folded newspaper section—and three feet away was a public trashcan! It was enough to make Iron Eyes tear up forlornly.

But there was reason to make the chief smile, too. At a different local park where weekend soccer games regularly leave the fields a littered mess, on Monday I saw a woman filling a trash bag with the shameful debris as she took her daily walk for exercise.

Two days later came a similar sight, this time a neighbor's garbage can with its overflowing contents stacked like a precarious game of Jenga. Not surprisingly, some of the trash toppled to the pavement.

Here is what was surprising: as I stood at the mailbox cluster a few houses down the street, the garbage man hopped out of his truck and quickly picked up the mess before driving on. He surely did not do so because he saw me watching, as I greatly doubt he had noticed me, but rather I am certain simply because he took pride in his job.

I say this confidently because a short while back I met a local garbage collector, now long retired, who shared some stories of his days as a "swamper"—that being the term for the worker who lifted and emptied the trash barrels into the truck by biceps before this chore became mechanized.

In the 1950s and '60s, swamping was backbreaking work as the curbside trash cans here were actually old steel oil drums weighing fifty-five pounds *empty*. Each swamper would hoist and dump about three hundred of these hernia-makers per shift.

"My back was plenty sore by the end of the day," the retired swamper told me. "But I actually enjoyed the work. We'd have races on the streets with another truck and whoever finished first, the other would buy lunch."

Being in such a rush you would expect this swamper might leave some emptied trash barrels strewn willy-nilly, surely not pausing to clean up any trash that fell wayside. You would be mistaken.

"I would never leave a barrel in the driveway so the person living there couldn't drive in," he explained. "And I'd never leave any trash for them to have to pick up. We took pride in our work."

In return, he continued, some customers showed

their appreciation by offering him hot coffee on cold mornings.

Note to self: I need to take a cup of coffee out to my garbage man next time the thermometer dips low. And I need to give a warm thank you to the woman at the nearby park next time I see her being a role model by keeping a small corner of America beautiful.

Twenty-Three

The Art of Excellence

——

WHILE spending an afternoon taking in the collection titled "Van Gogh to Munch" on temporary display at the Santa Barbara Museum, I could not help but think about the root canal I had a couple days earlier.

Do not be mistaken. This is not meant as a bitter review. Quite the contrary—I was awed by the oil-on-canvas *Lilacs* that Vincent van Gogh painted in 1887 and Claude Monet's *Villas in Bordighera* from three years earlier, to name just two masterpieces in the show.

The point is I was similarly impressed by the masterful handiwork of endodontist Dr. Timothy Jue, who turned my molar filled with molten lava into a calm, cool seascape, so to speak, performing the procedure so gently I nearly dozed off. Indeed, while perusing the "Van Gogh to Munch" masterworks it struck me that Dr. Jue is an artist who simply uses a different canvas, palette and brushes.

I saw my dentist, Dr. Stacy Schmitt, in the same light when he crafted and put in a gold crown. To be sure, the fabulous watercolors painted by his father that decorate Stacy's office are evidence of an artistic family gene.

These two open-mouth experiences opened my eyes. I began to see "art" in surprising places.

Even in parking spaces, such as when I watched a driver in a Honda Civic try to parallel park in a spot that looked challengingly tight. After backing in at the wrong angle and trying a forward-reverse-forward dance while drivers impatiently lined up behind him, he gave up and drove off. His failure made the artistry that followed all the more impressive when a woman in a SUV backed in perfectly (head turned, one hand on the steering wheel; no computerized automatic parking system) in one smooth swoop. It was performance poetry.

Speaking of poets, Robert Frost's famous "Mending Wall" came to mind when I witnessed, daily over the course of a week, progress as a skilled mason built a beautiful stone fence driveway entryway. Jigsaw puzzle pieces do not fit together more perfectly. "Something there is that doesn't love a wall," reads a line in Frost's poem, but it is hard to imagine anyone not appreciating the artistry of this wall.

Too, I love the artistry of the smooth stones that are stacked and balanced like dozens of Pacific snowmen in the new rock garden at Surfer's Point at the San Buenaventura State Beach. However, unlike snowmen, which are

96

typically three spheres tall with each smaller than the one below it, these rock star sculptures are five and seven and even ten stones tall, and often with larger pieces up high, defying imagination and seemingly the laws of physics. The gravity-defying surfers using their brightly colored boards to paint brushstrokes across the face of waves most certainly qualify as art as well.

Not far away on the bike path I witnessed more "art" of sorts when a serious cyclist suffered a flat back tire. Quicker than someone could balance a sculpture four or five stones high, he expertly repaired the flat with no cuss or greasy muss and was again pedaling away. If you are a cyclist it is surely no big deal; if you are not, it is art.

The South Swell Double India Pale Ale at Ventura Surf Brewing? The ravioli at Ferraro's Italian Restaurant? The desserts at Savory Café & Bakery? Art, art and art again.

Sport, too, is art as evidenced for example by the U.S. women's soccer team in the finals of the 2011 World Cup. That they lost to Japan, 3-1, in a penalty shootout after a 2-2 tie, was merely a cracked frame around a Monet. Indeed, the fast-break goal by SoCal's own Alex Morgan kicked through a keyhole at an angle Picasso would admire merits hanging on a velvet wall with a soft spotlight above. And the Rembrandt of a header by Abby Wambach was equally a brushstroke of genius.

More traditionally, an interesting and ambitious project recently completed by Ventura's Rima Muna and fellow artist Elizabeth Hudson from Paso Robles—"100 Drawings/Paintings In 100 Days"—is most certainly estimable art.

My son is studying abroad this summer and just sent a postcard home from a weekend trip to the Louvre. I wish I could have been there with him, but the truth is you do not have to travel far from wherever you are to find fine "art."

Twenty-Four

Riding to the Rescue

———

THIS is a love story.

It stars a boy and his grandfather, a thief and a school principal, Facebook and a village of caring people.

Tony, a fourth-grader at Mound Elementary in Ventura, had his bike stolen after leaving it at school overnight.

His misfortune mounted. Riding double on the crossbar of his grandfather's bike for the two-mile trip home from school shortly thereafter, Tony's foot caught in the spokes and he flew head over handlebars.

Todd Tyner, Mound's principal, had not known about the bike theft or the dangerous double-rides to and from school. When Tony showed up on crutches the next day, Tyner asked and learned and cared.

"I knew we needed to get Tony a replacement bike as soon as he was well enough to ride again," Tyner recalls thinking.

At 11:18 a.m. that very day, Tyner posted on his

Facebook page a brief summary of Tony's predicament. Shining the Bat-Signal above Gotham City's night skyline could not have elicited a speedier response of help.

Indeed, a mere two minutes later at 11:20 a.m.— sent from a mobile phone because the Good Samaritan did not want to delay until getting home—came this online reply: "I have a bike he can have. He can choose from 4 cuz my kids never ride them."

Another offer came at 11:36 a.m.—"He can have my beach cruiser. It needs fresh tires but that should be easy to take care of."

And another and another…

12:15 p.m. "I got $10. If we all chip in we can buy a nice new one."

12:21 p.m. "I have a specialized BMX I could part with! Needs a new pedal."

12:24 p.m. "I have 2 new bikes in my garage. Need air in tires."

2:24 p.m. "We have a brand new boys bike that he can have."

3:15 p.m. "I want to help. Can I drop some money off at school?"

And on and on, more than thirty offers for bikes, helmets, locks and cash in a few hours. The problem of no bike turned into one of too many bikes. A nice problem to have. Tyner actually had to turn off the Bat-Signal.

Sitting in his principal's office recalling the *It's A Wonderful Life*-like event, Tyner is asked if he was surprised by the kind outpouring?

"No, not really," he answers. "The Internet is a wonderful way to reach out to the community. I knew if I let people know about the need, someone would have an extra bike. This is a very caring community. I see it a lot."

This time it was a bike, but other days Tyner has seen backpacks and school supplies donated to kids who are without.

And this past December, Mound teachers collected two large bags of clothes and shoes for a couple students in need. They asked Tyner to surreptitiously drop them off at the boys' home before Christmas, which he did.

"We see them wearing the clothes," Tyner shares. "That is a rewarding feeling."

So, too, was the feeling of summoning Tony into the Principal's Office after the boy was finally off crutches three weeks later.

"I said, 'I know you need a bike,' " Tyner retells. "I told him about Facebook and that more than forty people had offered to help him out. Tony thought it was pretty exciting that there were people out there who cared enough to give him a bike."

Along with a new safety helmet and lock, Tony was given his choice of the two bikes that were ultimately donated—the other is being kept for a similar exigency down the road. He selected a shiny red BMX, good as new after Tyner cleaned it a little and pumped up the tires.

"Tony had a big smile when he rode home that day," Tyner says, beaming at the recent memory he will surely carry into his old age—as will Tony.

As I said at the start, this is a love story. The name of the bike benefactor is Danielle Love. How perfect is that?

Twenty-Five

Acts of Gold

——

THE other day I saw a most beautiful photograph, our iconic Ventura Pier captured moments after sunset with pastel clouds decorating the deep blue sky above a deeper blue ocean. The picture, taken by my talented friend Hank, epitomizes in a single frame why this is the Gold Coast.

The image also reminded me of Huell Howser, the iconic and beloved PBS host who passed away earlier this month, because it is a lovely example of the *California's Gold* his television show focused on.

Howser had a gift for chronicling famous landmarks and personalities, but his true genius was in storytelling about "ordinary" places and people who in truth were quite extraordinary. In his honor, here are four examples of Ventura County's Gold that at first thought would seem ordinary indeed: a folded newspaper, a trashcan, two cups of coffee, a child's toy.

Early each morning, without fail, the white-bearded gentleman walks a block from his home, turns left at the corner and at the first driveway picks up the newspaper that he then sets by the front door.

Asked about his un-random act of kindness, Rick answers that the woman living inside is elderly and has severe arthritis. His own mother had suffered similarly and he cannot bear the thought of this lady beginning her day with a painful short walk outside.

Hearing this makes my day more golden. As Huell might have said, "Amaaazzzing!"

Before sunrise every Wednesday, rainy or clear, "Lefty" as he is called by all who know him, rolls the trash barrel and recycling bin (or organic waste bin, depending on which is being collected) out to the curb.

This would not be unusual except Lefty does this chore for the neighbor directly across the street. What is more, his neighbor is neither elderly nor arthritic. In fact, Lefty's neighbor is supremely fit; he works out at the gym regularly and surfs religiously.

Lefty, now a vigorous seventy-seven, has been performing this altruistic deed for more than fifteen years, no matter that his neighbor is a quarter-century his junior with two sons who have grown into hale and strong teenagers easily capable of the task.

"I was just trying to be neighborly," Lefty answers when asked how this all began. "It's not a chore. I enjoy doing it. I guess I did it once when he was out of town and it just became a habit."

The habit includes putting the emptied trashcans away. "That's a pleasure, too," says Lefty. "I just think you should treat people the way you want to be treated."

Hearing this is a treat to my spirit, the epitome of turning trash into treasure. As Huell might have said, "Oh my goshhhh!"

One recent morning, as is this teacher's habit on her way to work, Elektra stopped at Starbucks. When she reached into her purse to pay the cashier, she was thwarted. No, she had not forgotten her wallet—there was simply no charge because the previous customer, a woman Elektra did not know, surreptitiously paid for her coffee.

Shortly thereafter, Elektra was again getting her morning java fix when the woman in line ahead of her had her credit card declined. You can guess what happened next.

"I paid for her," Elektra shares. "She was floored and so appreciative. This is not to pat myself on the back—it is just to remind us all to show each other kindness. Pay it forward. It feels good. It warms the heart."

Hearing this warms my heart. As Huell might have said, "Wonderfullllll!"

Rhiannon, a young woman of modest means, was similarly in line recently and opened her wallet to buy a thirty-five-dollar Star Wars toy for a young boy ahead of her in line. She did not know the boy. She did this for no other reason than to be supremely kind.

"He didn't have even close to enough money for it," Rhiannon shares, adding: "It was the greatest feeling in the world. I wish I was rich so I could do it more often. I think I was more excited than he was."

Hearing this enriches my day. As Huell might have said, "It doesn't get any better than this. California's Gold."

Golden as the Ventura Pier at sunset.

Twenty-Six

Roadside Heroes

——

THE scene was not unusual: a car was broken down, blocking a lane and causing traffic to congest behind it while trying to merge and go around. With every passing moment, and every impatient honk from passing cars, the stranded driver's anxiety surely rose.

What happened next was also not unusual: the anguished face broke into a smile of relief when a cavalryman arrived, not on a fast horse but in a powerful tow truck.

In this instance from a few days past, the tow truck driver had the high-performance-turned-no-performance convertible securely loaded and on its way to the repair shop in the time it took me to run a few laps around an adjacent soccer field. He even gave the stranded driver a lift.

Watching it all unfold, I was reminded of a welcomed lift I once got from a tow truck driver, as well as a few other times my spirits were buoyed to see one drive up. Perhaps never more so than one night in 1994—the Los Angeles Rams' final season in Southern California before moving to St. Louis. By the time I finished writing my column and left the press box, it was late and dark. And raining.

The parking lot was a ghost town. And my car battery was dead. A fellow writer tried to give me a jumpstart. My engine groaned tiredly, but would not turn over. This was before cell phones were common, so my press-box colleague offered to find a payphone on his way to the freeway and call my wife, who would then call AAA on my behalf.

Being given "the Anaheim Stadium parking lot" as an address is not a whole lot better than being told "next to the needle in a haystack," yet twenty minutes later a tow truck circled around the dark stadium and came my way.

Despite the cold downpour, I remember the tow truck driver's disposition as being sunny and warm—he even greeted me by offering me a cup of hot coffee. After his powerful battery got my car started on the first try, he reminded me to drive safely on the slick freeways; he said he expected to have a busy night.

Over the ensuring years, my wife and I have needed AAA assistance numerous times for dead batteries and flat tires (it is amazing how quickly and seemingly effortlessly—and with no scraped knuckles or swearing!—a

tow truck pro can change a tire) as well as cars that were stranded in the driveway for unknown reasons and needed to be towed to the dealership.

Then there was the time not long ago my car suddenly needed CPR on the 110 Freeway near Staples Center in downtown Los Angeles where the Lakers play. With a metallic coughing under the hood, accompanied by smoke smelling like a mix of burning rubber and oil, I managed to make it to an exit and coast down the off-ramp. Escaping a potential stranding on the freeway, I felt like a WWII fighter pilot who had nursed a bullet-riddled plane to a safe landing.

My unsung hero this time was Caesar, his name stitched in blue script on a white oval patch on his navy shirt. Riding in the passenger seat of his truck cab I learned he was a modern immigrant success story. Coming to America legally, Caesar worked diligently and now owned his own tow truck; sent money home to his parents and his wife's parents in Mexico; and all three of his children were college graduates.

According to GPS, the repair shop I wanted my car taken to was a good distance beyond my free coverage and the penalty would be fairly steep. No problem—Caesar used his local knowledge of shortcuts to get us there a fraction of a mile under the limit.

"I think I have the best job in the world because I

get to help people every day," Caesar told me before driving off.

Like the man in the stalled high-performance convertible—and surely just like all of us when we inevitably need a tow, or jumpstart, or flat tire changed in the rain—when spirits need lifting, I think tow truck drivers more than pull their weight.

Twenty-Seven

Getting Lost, Happily

———

"THROUGH my own efforts," John Steinbeck wrote in *Travels with Charley: In Search of America,* "I am lost most of the time without help from anyone."

Through my own travels, I have been lost many times with help from someone—my son.

Make no mistake, the mistakes have not all been his doing. He is, after all, part homing pigeon, part human compass. Even when he was small, we could enter a parking garage in a strange city in daylight, drive in dizzying circles searching for a space, then exit onto a different street in a blindfold of darkness and he knew his bearings.

Nonetheless, over the years we have had our Gilligan and Skipper moments. Most recently, last week when The Boy was home from college for spring break, we got lost in Salinas looking for The Steinbeck House restaurant.

Technology, not The Boy, was to blame as the GPS

directions app developed a "recalculating" stutter. Like Neil Armstrong coolly landing Apollo 11's Lunar Module manually, The Boy turned off the computer and trusted himself until finally: "Mission Control, the Prius has parked."

The half-hour travail was well worth it. The Queen Anne style Victorian house was built in 1897 and Steinbeck was born in the front bedroom (now the restaurant's reception area) five years later. In the early 1930s he wrote his first two novels—*The Red Pony* and *Tortilla Flat*—in the front upstairs bedroom overlooking the valley.

The 1962 Nobel Prize for Literature recipient's boyhood home was authentically restored and opened to the public for tours, and lunches, in 1974 and designated a Literary Landmark in 1995. As a writer, I was mesmerized. As a bonus, no museum anywhere serves a tastier chicken salad sandwich.

Our step back in time included stepping down into the cellar (now the gift shop) where two volunteer docents —who, as teens, might have read *The Grapes of Wrath* when it was first published in 1940—were befuddled by the computerized cash register and eventually calculated my purchase with pencil, paper and a sales tax chart.

The road trip extended to San Francisco where The Boy got lost in reverence inside an art gallery featuring a remarkable collection of Salvador Dali's work. The Boy so fell in love with art under the magical mentorship of Patti Post at Ventura High School that he minored in Painting in college. Our home now resembles an art show with his framed pieces throughout.

As usual, I wandered the gallery more quickly than The Boy. An aggressive salesperson, however, matched my pace even after I politely explained I was not looking to buy but was merely along for the ride with my artist son.

My favorite Dali on display was a beautiful ink drawing of his wife, Gala. I should probably mention it is a nude. In defense of my lingering gaze, I will also share that nude pieces always bring to mind a story The Boy tells about the evening one of his art classes at USC had a nude model...

... a hairy gentleman who, like The Steinbeck House docents, may have read *The Grapes of Wrath* in its first edition as the original owner.

As each student walked into the art studio, The Boy retells, their facial expression silently transformed into "The Scream" by Edvard Munch.

Out of curiosity I asked the saleswoman the price of the Dali nude. "Seventy-five thousand," came the answer and I didn't even blink, distracted from the stunning Gala by the mental image of those stunned college art students.

Eventually I found myself in a room dedicated to Picassos. The saleswoman followed, as did her questions, including this: "Are you a collector?"

"Oh, no," I replied, amused she would think I could afford anything in this pricey gallery, adding nonchalantly with a casual sweep of my hand towards wherever The Boy now was in the gallery: "Only *his* stuff."

Her eyes widened with thrill: "You have exquisite taste!"

Instantly I realized what had been lost in translation—she thought my gesture had been to signify Picasso's stuff, not my son's.

Thus another wonderful trip became even more so, for as Steinbeck also wrote in *Travels with Charley*—"One goes, not so much to see but to tell afterward."

Twenty-Eight

Commencement Address

——

"LADIES and gentlemen of the class of (2015): Wear sunscreen. If I could offer you only one tip for the future, sunscreen would be it. The long-term benefits of sunscreen have been proved by scientists whereas the rest of my advice has no basis more reliable than my own meandering experience. I will dispense this advice now."(1)

"The best advice I can give anybody about going out into the world is this: Don't do it. I have been out there. It is a mess."(2) "Don't ask what the world needs. Ask what makes you come alive, and go for it. Because what the world needs is people who have come alive."(3)

"Find your Passion with a capital P!"(4) "If you aren't fired with enthusiasm, you will be fired with enthusiasm."(5)

"The fireworks begin today. Each diploma is a lighted match. Each one of you is a fuse."(6) "Education is the most powerful weapon you can use to change the world."(7)

"You are educated. Your certification is in your degree. You may think of it as the ticket to the good life. Let me ask you to think of an alternative. Think of it as your ticket to change the world."(8)

"Never doubt that a small group of thoughtful, committed people can change the world—indeed that's the only thing that ever has."(9)

"Learn as if you were to live forever; live as if you were to die tomorrow."(10) "Share your knowledge. It is a way to achieve immortality."(11) "When you get, give; when you learn, teach."(12)

"The more that you read, the more things you will know. The more that you learn, the more places you'll go."(13) "Do not go where the path may lead; go instead where there is no path and leave a trail."(14) "Wherever you go, no matter what the weather, always bring your own sunshine."(15)

"What lies behind us and what lies before us are tiny matters compared to what lies within us."(16) "It takes courage to grow up and become who you really are."(17) "Always, always, always, always, always, always, always do the thing you fear and the death of fear is certain."(18)

"It is not the mountain we conquer but ourselves."(19) "One can have no smaller or greater mastery than mastery of oneself."(20)

"Wise are those who learn that the bottom line

doesn't always have to be their top priority."(21) "We make a living by what we get, we make a life by what we give."(22) "If you don't make an effort to help others less fortunate than you, then you're just wasting your time on Earth."(23)

"Do not judge each day by the harvest you reap, but by the seeds you plant."(24) "The true meaning of life is to plant trees, under whose shade you do not expect to sit."(25)

"Life is too short to wake up in the morning with regrets, so love the people who treat you right. Forget about the ones who don't, and believe that everything happens for a reason. If you get a chance, take it. If it changes your life, let it. Nobody said that it'd be easy, they just promised it would be worth it."(26)

"Twenty years from now you will be more disappointed by the things that you didn't do than by the ones you did do. So throw off the bowlines. Sail away from the safe harbor. Catch the trade winds in your sails. Explore. Dream. Discover."(27) "And will you succeed? Yes! You will indeed! 98 and 3/4 percent guaranteed."(28)

"There is a good reason they call these ceremonies 'commencement exercises'—graduation is not the end, it's the beginning."(29) "When you leave here, don't forget why you came."(30) "Don't cry because it's over. Smile because it happened."(31)

"When you leave home, you take home with you."(32)

———

(1-*Mary Schmich*. 2-*Russell Baker*. 3-*Howard Thurman*. 4-*Wayne Bryan*. 5-*Vince Lombardi*. 6-*Eward Koch*. 7-*Nelson Mandela*. 8-*Tom Brokaw*. 9-*Margaret Mead*. 10-*John Wooden*. 11-*Dalai Lama*. 12-*Maya Angelou*. 13-*Dr. Seuss*. 14-*Ralph Waldo Emerson*. 15-*Anthony J. D'Angelo*. 16-*Ralph Waldo Emerson*. 17-*e.e. cummings*. 18-*Ralph Waldo Emerson*. 19-*Edmund Hillary*. 20-*Leonardo da Vinci*. 21-*William Arthur Ward*. 22-*Winston Churchill*. 23-*Wayne Bryan*. 24-*Robert Louis Stevenson*. 25-*Nelson Henderson*. 26-*Bob Marley*. 27-*Mark Twain*. 28-*Dr. Seuss*. 29-*Orrin Hatch*. 30-*Adlai E. Stevenson*. 31-*Dr. Seuss*. 32-*Maya Angelou*.)

Twenty-Nine

Hall of Fame Wisdom

—

"WHEN I was eleven, my daddy taught me the greatest thing," George Anderson once told me. "Something that's so very important. He taught me that there's only one thing in your entire lifetime that's free. That's to be nice to people. It don't cost you nothing at all to be nice."

It was a lesson George, more famously known as "Sparky," learned well. My favorite personal memory of Sparky, who died at age seventy-six on Nov. 4, 2010, encapsulates his kindness.

As I drove up his street to meet him for an interview, I spotted Sparky finishing his morning walk in a curious manner: he kept detouring up and down his neighbors' driveways.

When he greeted me in his own driveway, Sparky explained he was taking the newspapers up to the front doors. In the evenings once a week he was happy to move others' trash barrels from the curb up the driveway as well.

It don't cost you nothing at all to be nice.

"If you were to go to dinner with me and the service was bad and you made a remark to the waiter or waitress, that would be the last time you had dinner with me," Sparky once told an audience at Cal Lutheran University. "You don't know what went on in the kitchen. We have the right not to go back to that restaurant, but not the right to humiliate another person."

It don't cost you nothing at all to be nice.

Three times Sparky managed his teams to World Series championships, but he was also a champion humanitarian. For example, in 1987 he created a foundation which to date has donated more than $4 million to Children's Hospital of Michigan and Henry Ford Hospital.

On perhaps the greatest baseball day of his life, the day he was voted into the Hall of Fame in 2000, Sparky shared with me sincerely, for he spoke no other way: "I love baseball dearly, but the foundation is the most important thing I ever did in my life. I can go to my grave with that. I love baseball, but you can't take baseball to your grave. Helping children is so much more important than baseball."

He always had his priorities as perfectly ordered as a lineup card for the Big Red Machine. This was again evident when he delivered the commencement address at Dorsey High School's 2001 graduation ceremony.

The last to speak following more than a half-hour's

worth of orators who had said a lot, and yet said very little, Sparky (Dorsey Class of 1953) stepped to the dais. In just seven minutes—remember, the Gettysburg Address was just 267 words long—he cut through all the pomp and circumstance with powerful substance.

Speaking without notes, Sparky did not speak without heart. "I would say to you that I'm very proud of you," he began, "but everyone says that. I don't want it that way. I want *you* to be proud of yourselves. I want you to look in the mirror and be proud of the person you see.

"There are two things I want you to do. I want you to go to bed at night and say this prayer: 'I am the most precious person on Earth.' And then repeat it when you wake up each morning. It's so important to be proud."

Never one to mistake statistics and salaries, pennants and plaques, for true success, Sparky continued: "Today 'success' has come to mean how much money you have; how big of a house; how fancy of a car you drive."

He shook his head. "That's not success."

It was not lip service. Despite having earned seven figures annually as a legendary manager, Sparky lived in the same modest home in Thousand Oaks for nearly four decades.

" 'Success' is what kind of a human being you are," he told the new graduates. "It is what I do as a person, how I act as a person, that is important. When they put you in that box at the end of your life, if you were a good person you will have been successful."

George "Sparky" Anderson was a Hall of Fame person.

Thirty

Zen Custodian

———

EACH holiday season the familiar song lyric *"It's the hap-peeee-est tiiiimmme of the year"* makes me think of Doug.

"Big Doug" as I called him, at his request. He is perhaps the *hap-peeee-est* grown-up I've ever met in my entire life.

Let me backtrack. For one holiday season and spring, when I was fresh out of college and awaiting post-graduate journalism school to begin, I did work through a temporary placement agency. I guess you could say I was a Kelly *Boy*.

My first temp assignment was a graveyard-shift gig typing information for an insurance company into a computer from ten p.m. until six in the morning. *Yaaawwwwwn.* (If your premiums mysteriously quadrupled without reason in February of 1982, I belatedly apologize for imputing erroneous data while sleepy.)

As you can imagine, when the temp agency had an opening to do some bookkeeping (pronounced "filing") at a bank, I jumped at the eight-to-five daylight hours. I also jumped into a barber's chair.

It was a bank job that even a future sports columnist could handle. I basically had eight hours to do four hours of mindless paperwork—and that's if I did not rush myself. (My editors ever since probably swear my work habits haven't sped up.)

Anyway, this left lots of time to visit Big Doug, who stood six-foot-something and weighed three-hundred-something pounds. Huge Doug was more like it.

Big Doug was the janitor of this six-story bank building in downtown Wilmington, Delaware. He had a slight limp due, in time I would find out, to circulatory problems caused by diabetes. Also, I learned, he had a history of heart problems. Not the healthy life most of us wish for.

And yet he was the *hap-peeee-est* person you will ever hope to meet.

I first met Big Doug when the Xerox machine on the third floor, where my office cubicle was located, broke down on my second day on the job. My supervisor gave me a pile of files that needed documents copied, directions and a hastily hand-drawn map, and the chore of going down four flights of stairs to the basement, through a labyrinth of halls that wound through a workshop area, to use the backup copier.

What a crummy task, right?

No, what great luck!

On my way back through the maze after making copies, I bumped into Big Doug in his workshop. He kindly offered me some coffee. I politely thanked him, but explained I wasn't a coffee drinker.

The next day when I passed through his workshop, Big Doug had a can of Coke waiting for me. "Here, son, rest your feet a spell," he said, pulling out a spare wooden chair.

Even after the third-floor copying machine was repaired, I kept going to the basement to make copies—and rest my feet a spell. Indeed, Big Doug would always have a cold Diet Coke waiting for me and I started to bring him a doughnut in return. His favorite was glazed old-fashioned. What an odd pair we made—a heavy-as-Hardy man with diabetes eating a sugary doughnut and a skinny-as-Laurel kid drinking a diet soda.

In a building full of stressed out suits and dress heels, overall-clad Big Doug in his well-worn work boots was as serene as a yoga instructor. I cannot recall even once seeing him without all thirty-two of his teeth on display. Nor did I ever hear anything but cheerful words come out of that smile. Mr. Zip-a-Dee-Doo-Dah with a hammer, pliers, dustpan and broom.

We would sit there, sometimes for a spell that

lasted half an hour—his workload was apparently as light as mine—resting our feet a little and talking a lot. Big Doug eating his old-fashioned doughnut and washing it down with coffee, and me drinking my can of Diet Coke. An African-American in his late fifties from a big eastern city (Philly) and a white kid in his early twenties from a small SoCal beach town (Ventura) with nothing in common.

Or, maybe, everything in common. Like, above all, a wish to be happy.

Big Doug's family made him happy. He talked all the time about his children, grown now and moved away but still close to his heart, and always his eyes and face lit up an extra hundred watts at their mention.

Fishing also made him happy. Big Doug had an old dinghy he liked to take out on a nearby lake. Sometimes his wife would join him, not to fish mind you, just to keep him company. He said they enjoyed each other's company, even after many, many years together. The key to a happy marriage, he told me, was easy: Be nice to each other.

Be nice. It sounds so simple, doesn't it?

Big Doug made happiness seem simple. Maybe for him it was. Maybe he was happy because he kept his life simple. Thoreau the Janitor. He had an eight-to-five job that he didn't take home with him. And he had a home to go to after work where someone whose company he enjoyed, and enjoyed his, was waiting each evening. And he had grown kids who phoned him often and visited when they could. Zip-a-Dee-Doo-Dah indeed.

When my life seems spinning a bit too quickly, with too much stress and too many worries, and too little fun and happiness, I often pause and rest my feet a spell and think of Big Doug, the Zen Custodian, whose mountaintop was in the bowels of a bank basement. It always makes me feel better.

Too, it makes me a little melancholy. You see, on my final day of assignment at the bank after working there nearly three months, I navigated my winding way down to the basement to say goodbye to Big Doug. But he wasn't in his workshop and was nowhere to be found. I checked repeatedly all day that last Friday. No warm friendly face, no cold Diet Coke. No chance to say farewell—and thanks.

I like to think my happy friend took the day off to go fishing with the enjoyable company of his wife.

Woody Woodburn

Thirty-One

Our Love Story

"QUIT joking around," the beautiful young woman said, her words followed by the music of her laughter.

Not exactly the response a guy hopes for when popping "The Question." Of course the proposal would have been taken more seriously had the young man been holding an engagement ring or at least gotten down on bended knee.

In truth, he had not planned to propose. But when his college sweetheart matter-of-factly said she was planning to move to wherever he did following his graduation the following month, he replied without thought or hesitation: "Well, then, let's get married."

After she stopped laughing, he tried once more: "I'm serious. Will you marry me?"

What an idiot he was to ask. And she a greater fool surely to answer, "Yes." After all, they were much too young to wed and have it endure: he was still a couple weeks shy of turning twenty-two and she just twenty-three

128

and a year out of college. They had dated for barely a year and a half—and that is not subtracting a three-month breakup (as mentioned, he was an idiot) in the middle of their romance, plus the previous summer spent apart.

Oh, yes, and he had never even met the girl's mother. You can just imagine how well the bride-to-be's long-distance phone call home with news of the engagement went over. Understandably, her parents living three thousand miles away tried to talk her into pushing the wedding date back a year from the just-around-the-corner October to the following September. The daughter compromised: she agreed on early September, which was more convenient for her schoolteacher mother's schedule— but the *upcoming* September, just four months hence.

Against all odds, and to my in-law's rightly amazement, my wife and I have now celebrated thirty-three wedding anniversaries. You would think this gives me some insight into what makes for a blissful marriage. Here, on men's behalf, is the best I can come up with:

Find a former high school homecoming princess whose outward beauty runs deep to a kind soul and caring heart; who is loving and confident and intelligent, charming and generous and strong; who has a sense of humor and an aura of grace; and, importantly, is foolish enough to happily marry someone not within a ZIP Code of being worthy of her hand.

Thirty-three years—and two children raised to adulthood—is a long time, yet it can also seem to have passed in about thirty-three days. The French writer Andre Maurois noted, "A happy marriage is a long conversation that always seems too short." Marry a woman who makes you feel thus.

Too, marry one who brings to my mind the poetry of Tennyson: "If I had a flower for every time I thought of you... I could walk through my garden forever."

If only I had memorized and recited those syrupy lines when I proposed it would have compensated for not having already bought an engagement ring. Actually, she would surely have laughed even more heartily at such lovesick tomfoolery.

In truth and in hindsight, I wish at that memorable moment I had quoted a passage from A.A. Milne's *Winnie-the-Pooh* for it describes how I have felt about Lisa almost since the night we met under mistletoe at a college Christmas party:

" 'We'll be Friends Forever, won't we, Pooh?' asked Piglet.

" 'Even longer,' Pooh answered."

Thinking back to our meet-cute, she in a light blue turtleneck sweater, a line from Shakespeare's *As You Like It* also springs to mind: "Who ever loved that loved not at first sight?" So it was with me.

Today the sight of my wife additionally evokes this couplet from *Hamlet*: "Love is begun by time, / And time qualifies the spark and fire of it."

As I reminisce about the spark and fire of seeing "Leese" walk down the aisle of Ventura's Community Presbyterian Church, the words of the great John Steinbeck seem most appropriate. In his essay "The Golden Handcuff" about his long and deep love for San Francisco, he wrote: "My God! How beautiful it was and I knew then how beautiful."

My God! How beautiful she was and I knew it then. I know it still.

Thirty-Two

Season of Love Stories

——

"TO every thing there is a season," Ecclesiastes 3 tells us, "and a time to every purpose under the heavens."

For my wife and me, the time of recent has been wedding season.

Nieces' weddings. Children of our friends' weddings. Weddings of co-workers young enough to be our children. Our children's friends' weddings. Owen Wilson and Vince Vaughn don't go to as many ceremonies in *Wedding Crashers* as we have the past year.

Our own wedding was thirty-three years ago and there was no video made of the ceremony and the reception was a blur and quite honestly I would like a do-over.

By this I do not mean a do-again by renewing our vows in front of new friends and family we have gained since our own first "I do"—although this, too, would be wonderful.

Rather, I would like to relive our original wedding with the same bridal party and same groomsmen and the same entire guest list. "Groundhog Day" on September 4, 1982.

Given a magical do-over, I would make a better effort to stop and smell the bridal bouquet, so to speak, and savor more specific moments and memorize more priceless interactions from the day.

Indeed, after watching my beautiful bride walk down the aisle to meet me at the pulpit, everything else—the verse readings, the minister's words, our vows and our first kiss as husband and wife, the giddy walk-on-air back down the aisle together, the reception line, toasts given, our first dance, even how a groomsman wound up in a swimming pool in his tux—is pretty much all lost in the fog of time.

Better than renewing our vows, it seems to me, is now going to weddings. Sitting in a church pew or nestled around a gorgeous garden spot or overlooking the ocean or a scenic country club fairway, allows one to experience the circumstance and pomp and importance of the moment much more clearly than can the two people standing front and center—and nervous and excited and overwhelmed and overjoyed.

Being a wedding spectator offers the chance to vicariously be the groom or bride again with the advantage of not being bowled over by the occasion. It entices you to silently renew your own vows and commitment as you watch the celebrated couple do so.

Indeed, if you are married, it is almost impossible not to be affected watching two others join the club of matrimony. The next time you are at a wedding, when the bride is saying her vows slyly take a quick peek around and notice how many married couples in attendance reach down and squeeze each other's hands; after the big kiss, see how many little kisses among married spectators follow.

Here is something else rejuvenating about attending someone else's wedding. Even if I happen to already know the answer, I still like to ask the blissful couple about their "meet-cute." It is always, and I do mean always, a story they light up in retelling.

Too, listening always, and again I do mean always, lightens my heart and reminds me of my own magical first encounter that led to "for better and for worse, in sickness and in health."

Like weddings, Valentine's Day offers a similar opportunity to be inspired by young love. If you go for a walk along the beach today, or out to a restaurant tonight, you will have no trouble picking out the couples on dates and newlyweds.

Equally heartening are the couples that appear to be newly in love or newly married, but at the same time you can just tell they have actually been together for a long time. If there were a polite way to do so, I would love to interrupt them briefly and ask how they met and also for their secret to making the magic last.

I have a hunch some of these lovebirds might mention that going to a lot of weddings helps keep their own marriage happy and fresh.

In this season of my life, that's one thing I would say.

Thirty-Three

Yosemite on a Grander Scale

BEFORE embarking on a new travel adventure it is my habit to read a book or two about the destination. So it was I picked up *Letters from Alaska* by famed naturalist John Muir chronicling his 1879 and 1880 explorations of the southeastern Last Frontier.

Finishing the final chapter before landing in Anchorage, it was clearly obvious Muir was guilty of gross hyperbole, perhaps vested in selling timeshare igloos in Glacial Bay. How else to explain the theme of his "letters" for the San Francisco *Daily Evening Bulletin* basically calling the Yosemite Valley the ugly stepsister of princess Alaska.

"The clouds cleared away," Muir wrote of Glacier Bay, "and we had glorious views of the ice-rivers pouring down from their spacious fountains on either hand, and of the grand assemblage of mountains immaculate in their robes of new snow, and bathed and transfigured in the most impressively lovely sunrise I ever beheld."

Also: "This is your Yosemite, only this is on a

grander scale."

Grander than Half Dome? With lovelier sunrises? Actually, yes and yes again. If anything, Mr. Yosemite was understating the marvels of our forty-ninth state.

Audrey Sutherland, author of the terrific newly released *Paddling North* (published by Patagonia Books) chronicling her eight hundred and fifty-mile solo kayaking trip from Ketchikan to Skagway, Alaska, agrees: "Night does not fall. It rises from earth as the sun sinks low, sets, and embraces the land with its shadow. How could I describe this place? Words could only be read and the scene imagined. Even a photo could only be seen."

Too, she writes: "As the song said, there was nowhere else on earth that I would rather be." High praise from a native Californian who has lived in paradise Hawaii for sixty years.

For the seven days I recently spent traveling the Inside Passage, including Ketchikan, I fully agreed. Most especially, for forty minutes there was nowhere else on earth I would rather have been than flying over five glaciers outside Juneau.

The nearest comparison I can offer is when at age ten I saw the ocean for the first time and a day later rode Disneyland's Matterhorn. Sitting in the co-pilot's seat of an eight-passenger seaplane as Dan flew us over Muir's "grand assemblage of mountains" and then breathtakingly skimmed above 3,000-year-old glaciers named Norris, Taku, Hole-In-The-Wall, and East Twin and West Twin was an E-ticket ride on steroids.

Because of its crystalline structure formed under high pressure, glacier ice absorbs all colors but blue, which it reflects. Hence the ice of a "calving" glacier where chunks break free and fall into the sea is remarkably blue. In fact, I have never seen a richer, deeper, purer, bluer blue.

While witnessing a glacier from sea level is truly impressive, from above the "glorious views of the ice-rivers," to use Muir's apt description, defy description. Or, to paraphrase Sutherland, words can only be read and the scene imagined. Photos can only be seen. In the cockpit of a tiny prop plane the grandeur can be *felt*.

And it felt, I dare say, grander than Yosemite Valley.

After our seaplane "landed" on water, I asked Dan if he ever grows jaded of the scenes he just shared with us. Rubbing the lumberjack's ginger beard covering a square granite jaw, he answered: "Not yet. It's still awesome and beautiful every time I fly over it."

After a moment's reflection, Dan added: "But I've only been doing it six or seven times a day for fourteen years."

In other words, there is nowhere else on earth he would rather be.

While Muir urged "Go, go and see" Alaska while Sutherland writes of the land, "Here the sunset goes on and on, hours of shading through gold to rose to mauve," it says here this cannot match the Monet palettes of the sun sinking into the Pacific Ocean alongside the Channel Islands.

Indeed, ask me at such a grand moment where I would rather be and I will answer every time: "Nowhere else on earth."

Thirty-Four

High Cost of Pretty Toys

"OUR inventions are wont to be pretty toys, which distract our attention from serious things," wrote Henry David Thoreau. "They are but improved means to an unimproved end."

By this I think HDT—why spell it out when you can "simplify, simplify" by using a time-saving acronym? —could have been referring to email, Twitter, Instagram, blogs and the Internet in general 150 years ahead of his time.

Time-saving is a joke, though not a LOL one. It is ironic, really—email is much speedier than postal mail and yet in the unimproved end actually takes up more time. I say this after having gone on vacation for the first time in the Internet Age without taking along my laptop. Add in spotty-at-best smartphone coverage and sky-high roaming rates, and for nine days on a cruise ship I was unconnected.

The Alaskan Inside Passage was my Walden Pond.

I do not consider myself an Internet junkie. Except

for select email and text messaging, and checking a sports score now and then, I largely use my smartphone as a dumb phone. It isn't a bionic appendage or my companion at the dinner table and parties.

So I was surprised when I suffered Internet withdraw after just forty-eight hours without connection: "Hello, my name is Woody and I am an megabyte addict."

The desire to text message family and friends grew each day. I desperately wanted to look up the daily match results of Mike and Bob Bryan's march to the U.S. Open championship and their record-breaking twelfth Grand Slam title.

And, of course, I craved to check email.

Yet I did not realize how much time I spent online until I got reconnected after going cold turkey in the Alaskan cold. My inbox alone was an eye-opener. Clicking and deleting all the obvious junk email unopened took more than twenty minutes. Deleting others that required opening before determining they were trash filled up the rest of the hour.

Add the emails that required reading but no reply; those meriting quick responses; and others calling for lengthier thoughtful comment, and my first day back in the digitalized world was spent playing in-box catch up.

I felt a little like Sisyphus, who in Greek lore was punished by being forced to push a boulder up a mountain

—only to have it roll back down, thus forcing him to repeat the labor for eternity. My boulder was email; no sooner did I whittle down my inbox when new arrivals increased the total once again. I was Lucy frantically trying to keep pace with the chocolates as the conveyor belt keeps speeding up.

I did not even attempt to get caught up reading the news blogs I favor and Twitter users I follow, informative and entertaining as they are. To do so would surely have taken another full day. I should add, this vacation was shortly before I joined the time-sucking-black-hole called Facebook.

While much of my reading and corresponding online is valuable and educational and necessary, I have to admit some of it is quite the opposite. In fact, after having been unplugged my conservative guesstimates is I waste an hour a day on my laptop and smartphone. This calls to mind another HDT gem: "It is not enough to be busy. So are the ants. The question is: What are we busy about?"

I need to reevaluate what I am busy about.

As my good friend and great mentor, Wayne Bryan, points out during his national speaking engagements, in the time an average American spends watching TV—six to eight hours daily according to numerous surveys—over the course of a year, he or she could learn to play a musical instrument *and* speak a foreign language *and* read a handful of classic books (or write a book). In fact, Wayne further insists, in the wasted commercial time alone we could do one of the above.

Here is my take-away from my laptop/smartphone sabbatical: I want to be less busy on the Internet. This is not to say I am becoming a Luddite. Technology is both wondrous and wonderful. Still, I am going to keep in mind one more thought by Henry David Thoreau: "The price of anything is the amount of life you exchange for it."

In other words, even free Internet access and unlimited data cell plans come with high roaming costs.

Thirty-Five

The Art of Appreciation

—

AS you were drifting off to sleep during the recent storms, did you hear the nighttime raindrops dancing on your rooftop?

I mean *really* hear nature's symphony? To these ears, a Mozart piano concerto was never lovelier.

And after the clouds cleared did you see the Monet-like brushstrokes left behind on our mountains? To be honest, I missed them until a friend shared an encounter she had during her daily morning walk.

Standing smack-dab in the middle of the street in her Southern California neighborhood was a man she had never before seen. Her first thought was, "What is he doing?" And a second: "I hope he doesn't get run over."

As she passed, the man said, "I was just taking a moment before work to appreciate the snow on the mountains. We just moved here." With that he climbed into his truck and drove off, his day off to a grander start than had he been in a hurried rush.

As my friend noted afterwards: "We hear all the time about gratitude; appreciation for little things; things we take for granted. Find them—just don't get hit by a car!" Sometimes we all need reminders of our blind spots, our deaf spots, of things—both little and large—we take for granted. We need fresh counsel on an old maxim by Walter Hagen: "Don't hurry. Don't worry. You're only here for a short visit. So don't forget to stop and smell the roses."

Also, stop and look at the snow on the mountains.

"The journey is better than the inn," is how Cervantes poetically put this Zen-like ideal in the 17th century.

Much more recently in *Zen and the Art of Motorcycle Maintenance: An Inquiry into Values*, first published in 1974, Robert M. Pirsig wrote about climbing a mountain and how too many people focus only on reaching its summit:

"When you're no longer thinking ahead, each footstep isn't just a means to an end but a unique event in itself. *THIS* leaf has jagged edges. *THIS* rock looks loose. These are things you should notice. To live only for some future goal is shallow. It's the sides of the mountain which sustain life, not the top. Here's where things grow."

Here's where things grow, indeed, and life's sustaining pleasures happen.

Here's where mountains are frosted with snow.

Here's where children laugh on a merry-go-round

and smile as melting ice cream drips down their chins.

Here's where children scream with delight when a rogue wave crashes into a sandcastle.

Here's firefly-like sparks rising above a glowing campfire.

Here's a child's kite and a Monarch butterfly both dancing on a shared breeze.

Here's where the shade beneath the canopy of a magnificent oak is perfect for reading or napping or daydreaming.

Here's a seagull gracefully suspended without even flapping its wings.

Here's a father running alongside as his young daughter learns to ride a two-wheeler, the girl unaware her dad is no longer holding the seat to provide balance.

Here's a speedy mother pushing a jogging stroller, both faces joyous.

Here's noticing the new beauty in a loved one's face you have stared at a million times before.

Here's a friend's smile and a dog's tail wag.

Here's the Ventura Pier, in its own way as majestic as the Eiffel Tower.

Here's the Channel Islands, as beautiful as Yosemite's Half Dome.

Here's wildflowers blossoming in springtime and stars doing likewise at nighttime.

Here's a boy tracking mud inside and a Zen-like mother wise enough to know she will too soon miss his messes.

Here's a grade-schooler's painting, as imaginative and wonderful as anything by Picasso, held by magnets on a refrigerator door.

Here's a balletic surfer using the face of a wave as her stage.

Here's Two Trees standing sentinel in evening silhouette.

Here's "young love" walking hand-in-hand along the beach—and old lovers doing so, too.

Here's the arrival gate at the airport.

Here's an inspiring sunrise and a clear sunset, and also here's thunderclouds and a rainbow afterwards.

Here's where memories grow.

Here's a reminder to take time to look at the snowcapped mountains, taste the strawberries in wintertime, and smell all of the "roses" along life's artful journey.

Thirty-Six

Lesson from Sri Lanka

GRADUATION season is upon us and among those who will fling their mortarboards skyward in celebration this year is my youngest nephew from Camarillo High School. Here is my commencement address written personally for him with the hope others may find wisdom and inspiration as well.

Congratulations, Rhett. Before continuing on your educational expedition and life journey, I want to tell you about the banana knife your cousin brought home from Sri Lanka last year as a gift for me.

The curved eight-inch blade is not burnished smooth except for its sharp edge, yet it is still beautiful for its utility—it can cut a banana bunch from a tree, chop down bamboo stalks, slice open a letter with equal ease. In today's world, having a wide range of skills will serve you well.

Conversely, its lacquered native dark hardwood handle is art to behold—and hold. Adding to the sublimity is that your cousin watched the master blacksmith fashion this handiwork in an hour's time.

Greg also saw craftswomen weave strands of colorfully dyed palm leaves into wondrous purses of varying patterns. Meanwhile, from earthen clay other artists created pots and bowls that are equally useful and attractive.

These Sri Lankan artisans, it seems to me, serve as an instructive metaphor. Each day we all receive twenty-four hours, like a new chunk of raw clay or a pile of palm fronds or a piece of metal. Our challenge and duty is to use our vision, talents, and perseverance to create something meaningful.

Too, Rhett, I wish to share a story from a trip Greg took a few years earlier to the tiny village of Sikoro in Mali, Africa. Because his luggage was lost, and because he had neglected to pack anything in his carry-on bag for just such a mishap, he spent two weeks with only the clothes on his back.

Yet instead of calamitous, the lost luggage actually proved to be serendipitous because he got a life lesson in experiencing how his impoverished hosts make do with very few possessions.

The people of Sikoro live in mud-brick huts, sleep on woven mats atop hard dirt floors and pump water from wells. They often lack enough fruits and vegetables. Most do not have shoes. And yet despite what to us seems a hardscrabble existence, they are extremely happy.

They smile constantly, laugh easily, dance freely. Worries about car payments and job promotions do not weigh on their minds. They may not have much materially by our standards, but by theirs they have enough and feel rich in experiences and community.

Rhett, you would do well to pack some of these values of the Sikoro villagers in your luggage, so to speak, as you travel life's roads.

Speaking of packing, Rhett, I wish to close with a scene from the book *Repacking Our Bags* by Richard Leider. He was on a backpacking trek in Africa and the group's Maasai guide, Koyie, traveled with only a spear and a stick for cattle-tending. Leider, on the other hand, was outfitted with a backpack stuffed with "necessities."

After they made camp the first evening, Leider laid out all his fancy gear. He writes:

"I unsnap snaps, unzip zippers, and un-Velcro Velcro. From pockets, pouches, and compartments, I produce all sorts of strange and wonderful items. Eating utensils, cutting devices, digging tools. Direction finders, star gazers, map readers. Things to write with, on, and for. Various garments in various sizes for various functions. Medical supplies, remedies, and cures. Little bottles inside little bottles inside little bottles. Waterproof bags for everything. Amazing stuff!

"I look over at Koyie to gauge his reaction," Leider continues. "He seems amused but he is silent. Finally, after several minutes of just gazing at everything, Koyie turns to me and asks very simply, but with great intensity: 'Does all this make you happy?' "

Pursue happiness, Rhett, but pursue it wisely. As Patagonia founder Yvon Chouinard has sagely said: "The more you know, the less you need."

Thirty-Seven

Reading the Fine Print

I cannot tell a lie: George Washington biographers, United States historians, and the History Channel have some revisions to make.

This is specifically so regarding the famous speech General Washington gave on March 10, 1783, to the Continental Army in Newburgh, New York, at the close of the Revolutionary War.

Addressing grievances over the failure of Congress to honor its promises to the troops regarding salary and pensions, Washington's initial words were not well received by his men. He then took out a letter from a member of Congress explaining the government's financial difficulties and, with squinting eyes, began reading. Suddenly the great leader stopped, reached into his coat pocket and took out a pair of reading glasses—few even knew he wore readers.

"Gentlemen," Washington resumed, "you will permit me to put on my spectacles, for I have not only grown gray but almost blind in the service of my country."

Historians note that Washington's men were deeply moved with renewed affection, some even brought to tears, by the vulnerability of this "aging" and "old" warrior. As a result the officers cast a unanimous vote accepting the rule of Congress and keeping alive the American experiment.

My bone to pick with historical experts is the use of "old" and "aging."

Washington was but fifty-one!

My exact age as I write this!

The thing is, *of course* Washington needed spectacles—estimates are more than ninety percent of people over age forty need reading glasses. And basically no one over age fifty can read the statistics about the percentage of people over fifty who need reading glasses, without reading glasses.

When I turned forty and had no problem reading the fine-print eye chart, my optometrist Dr. Tom Funnell expressed casual surprise. After three or four more annual visits, he was duly impressed and made a professional mistake: he offhandedly mentioned he had had only one patient make it to age fifty without needing readers.

My wife will tell you that of all my countless faults, being overly competitive ranks No. 1. It used to only rank second, so I worked diligently to raise it.

Sneakily, my much-better-half employs this streak against me by mentioning things like, "So-and-so's husband is the best dishwasher emptier in town." When I told her what Dr. Tom said, she knew I would be reading books in Braille if need be until I turned fifty in order to claim bragging rights.

After three decades of marriage she knows me too well; I squinted my way to fifty-one before finally admitting to Dr. Tom at my last appointment that I needed to be fit with readers.

The past few years I was stubbornly kidding myself. First, I found I could only read the phonebook in good light.

Books and newspapers were next, although for a while I checked this off to new energy-efficient light bulbs that clearly aren't as bright as their wattages claim.

Then I started increasing the font size of documents on my computer screen.

All the while I kept thinking to my hardheaded self, "I'll show you, Dr. Tom!"

And so, like a four-year-old insisting between yawns he isn't tired, I denied the obvious even as familiar restaurants grew dimmer and the print in menus became smaller.

The final straw came at dinner with friends when I had three choices: point to items on the microfilm menu, like a tourist in a foreign land who doesn't know the language, and ask the waiter to interpret; order last and simply get whatever sounded best from the options the three others selected; or borrow my wife's reading glasses.

Bringing to mind a "Seinfeld" episode where George winds up with women's frames for his eyeglasses, I chose the latter. The good news is I clearly spotted scallops and pasta listed in fine print, and it was excellent.

I got my own readers—professorial round-rimmed, tortoise shell, good-looking I think—a short while ago and I can again read the phonebook in near darkness and restaurant menus in candlelight; regular newsprint looks like headlines; and I do not need to hold my smartphone at arm's length to read a text or email.

I cannot tell a lie: I should have acted my age a number of years ago.

Thirty-Eight

Batman v Adam

—

SOCIAL media was all a-Twitter with outrage earlier this week when it was announced Ben Affleck has been cast as Batman in the upcoming *Man of Steel* movie sequel titled *Batman v Superman: Dawn of Justice*.

As someone who routinely wore Bat Gloves complemented by a bath towel safety-pinned around my neck to kindergarten, I am steamed that Batman is guest starring in a Superman movie rather than the other way around.

But here is what really got my Bat Tights in a twisted bunch—the fact that my mom long ago tossed out the Batman and Robin lunchbox I used in first grade. On eBay these lunchboxes produced in 1966, the year the *Batman* TV series debuted, are now collectibles selling for more than $200—double that if the Thermos is still intact. The fact that any of the Thermoses have survived nearly five *decades* boggles my mind because I am fairly certain I dropped mine and shattered its glass liner within five *days*.

The lunchbox itself was far more durable. This was a good thing because while Batman had to contend with the Joker, Riddler, and Penguin, my super villain was Adam—a lunch-stealing black lab about the size of a grizzly bear who lived along my walking route to Windermere Elementary School in Upper Arlington, Ohio.

I should point out that my mom packed my lunch pretty much every school day of my elementary life. That is roughly 1,100 lunches. All of them, I believe, were Oscar Meyer bologna on white Wonder Bread along with either two Hostess Ho-Ho's or one larger foil-wrapped Ding-Dong.

My great friend Dan Means' mom, meanwhile, always packed him a peanut butter and grape jelly sandwich and Fritos. One memorable day in first grade, Dan had trouble opening the mini-bag of corn chips. His frustration growing, Dan gripped the opposite sides of the bag extra tightly and gave a mighty Frito Bandito-like tug and…

… *RIPPP! Whoosh!* The entire sealed seam at the top gave way, sending Fritos flying everywhere, high and far, like confetti shot from a cannon after the final game of the NBA Finals. A few Fritos even got caught in the long florescent light fixtures high overhead that looked like ice-cube trays turned upside-down.

In my entire life I have yet to meet someone with a

better laugh than Dan's—it was half-cackle and half-emergency-asthma attack—and while he always used it freely, he never used it more enthusiastically than at that very moment.

Adam, however, was no laughing matter. I cannot tell you how many times I was lunch-jacked by him on my walk to school, though an estimate of two dozen might be on the shy side.

The first couple times Adam confronted me, I tried freezing in my tracks and commanding him to stop. This was as pointless as asking a mugger to put his gun away and leave nicely. The best thing to do was drop your lunch and run like hell before Adam knocked you over while taking it. Trying to outrun Adam from the get-go was futile. My older brothers, meanwhile, safely kept their lunches because they only had to outrun me, not Adam.

You might think my bologna sandwich and Ho-Ho's were safe inside my metal Batman lunchbox. You would be wrong. Like Grizzlies in Yellowstone Park that can open car doors to get food inside, Adam managed to unlatch it. I reckon Adam could have cracked a bank safe if there were Ho-Ho's inside.

Even kids who did not have to walk or ride their bikes past Adam's house on the way to school were not safe from his lunch-jackings. Like a hungry dragon, if Adam was not sufficiently fed he came looking for villagers.

Adam routinely got loose and roamed the mile from his yard to school before the morning bell rang. At the sight of him the playground would erupt in frenzied terror. Screaming kids scattered this way and that like panicked citizens in a Godzilla movie or fleeing beachgoers in *Jaws*.

After each incident, teachers would tally up the casualties and the principal would phone the mom of the family who owned Adam. Mrs. Young would then make, pack and bring the required number of replacement lunches to school.

To be honest, except for the trauma of it, having your lunch stolen by Adam actually was not so bad—it was sort of a badge of honor. Plus, Mrs. Young usually packed homemade chocolate-chip cookies.

Thirty-Nine

Meeting Stan Smith

NEARLY two decades before fictional Iowa farmer Ray Kinsella built his "Field of Dreams," a Court of Dreams was laid down in the middle of an Ohio cornfield for the inaugural 1970 Buckeye Open—now the ATP Western & Southern Open in Cincinnati.

The green hardcourt was built and they came: Arthur Ashe, Charles Pasarell, Bob Lutz, an aging Pancho Gonzales, and that year's eventual singles champion, Tom Gorman.

However, it was Lutz's doubles partner out of the University of Southern California, Stan Smith, who made the quickest—and most lasting—impression upon me.

I was a ten-year-old rookie ball boy working the very first match of the pro tournament. Like Smith, my forte was at net where I was quick and confident. But unlike the tall, lanky, blond Californian, I was not falling prey to my own miscues. The opening set was over quickly, as Smith did not win a single game.

In the second set, however, the three-time All-American from USC and 1968 NCAA singles champion found his form. Unleashing aces instead of double faults, put-away volleys and laser-guided passing shots instead of unforced errors, Smith won the second set as fleetly as he had lost the first. Ray Ruffels, a lefty out of Australia, suddenly became Ray *Ruffled* as Smith ran out the match. Final score: 0-6, 6-0, 6-0.

Walking off the court, my new idol paused to sign "Good luck, Stan Smith" on the brim of my tennis hat. A week later I got more than an autograph. I scored one of Smith's rackets—a custom Wilson Jack Kramer Pro Staff model, weighted "Heavy" with an oversized 4-7/8 grip.

On match point of the doubles final, Smith hit an overhead a fraction high of the sweet spot and the wooden racket head collapsed like a dry leaf. Still, the shot had enough power to win the point and give the title to Smith and Lutz.

Before shaking hands with their opponents at the net, Smith handed me his splintered racket. It was like having Babe Ruth give you a cracked bat before his home-run trot.

Behind a serve that came out of the treetops and a net game so monstrous that Romanian star Ilie Nastase nicknamed him "Godzilla," the mustachioed Smith soon rose to No. 1 in the world. He won the 1971 U.S. Open. He won Wimbledon in 1972. He won the prestigious year-end WCT Finals twice.

Too, Smith was Mr. Clutch in Davis Cup play, going 15-5 in singles and 20-3 in doubles (13-1 with Lutz) while setting a record by personally clinching the Cup five times.

Stanley Roger Smith was inducted into the International Tennis Hall of Fame in 1987 but his credentials date back to The Ojai Tennis Tournament "Where Champions Are Discovered" and where he won the 1964 Boys' Interscholastic Singles title and added three Collegiate Singles crowns, two Collegiate Doubles titles and one Open Doubles championship.

More than a half-century after his first appearance at The Ojai, Smith returned for 115th edition of the prestigious event in 2015 as its legend honoree.

"The main goal, of course, was to play on the main Libbey Park courts," Smith, now sixty-eight, recently recalled. "That was really special."

The Pasadena native who resides in Hilton Head Island, South Carolina, where he runs his own junior tennis academy, continued: "And the orange juice stand was the other highlight. It's funny how certain things stand out in your mind."

Funny indeed. When he was losing that six-love set to Ray Ruffels, this is what stands out in my mind: Stan

Smith argued a line call, that had gone in *his* favor, and ultimately prevailed in giving the point to his opponent.

I think of that whenever I look at that broken keepsake racket hanging on my wall to this day.

Forty

Stan Smith Sequel

PREVIOUSLY, I shared my cherished memory of being a ten-year-old ball boy for Stan Smith in 1970, two years before he would ascent to being ranked No. 1 in the world. After literally smashing his wooden racket while hitting an overhead smash on match point to win the doubles title with Bob Lutz, Smith gave me the crumpled frame as a souvenir.

To borrow the signature phrase from the late, great radio broadcaster Paul Harvey, "And now the rest of the story…"

In April of 2015, I had the good fortune to be a guest at "An Evening With Stan Smith" fundraising dinner held at the spectacular home of Valerie and Alan Greenberg to honor the former champion during the 115th annual Ojai Tennis Tournament.

In addition to my lovely wife, Lisa, I brought along that old broken Wilson Jack Kramer Pro Staff model racket. I have always regretted not asking Smith to autograph it that long-ago summer day in Ohio.

In Ojai, on a spring night, I now hoped to remedy that.

"Hello Mr. Smith. I'm Woody and we met forty-five years ago," I said as introduction. "I was a ball boy at the Buckeye Boys Ranch tournament."

"I remember you," Smith warmly joked. "You've grown a little taller since then."

It can be a dicey thing meeting one's hero. The risk is that in person he or she will fall shy of the image you hold. My boyhood idol measured up even in my adulthood, which is saying something because Smith stands six-foot-four.

For the next fifteen minutes, Smith, still five-set-trim at age sixty-eight, regaled me one-on-one with stories of his Hall-of-Fame career. Of Wimbledon, where he slept in a narrow bed a foot too short for him en route to winning the singles title in 1972.

Of his days at the University of Southern California, where he won the 1968 NCAA singles championship and partnered with USC teammate Lutz—who was also on hand this night—to capture two NCAA doubles crowns.

And of Davis Cup play, specifically his match for the ages in 1972 in Bucharest against Ion Tiriac, against eight Romanian line judges, against a head umpire intimidated by the hostile home crowd, against death threats on the U.S. players.

Tiriac's "out" balls were routinely called in and Smith's "in" shots called out. Smith actually got *two* such bad calls on *one* crucial point: Tiriac's shot landed a foot beyond the baseline but the line judge kept quiet; Smith, now playing every ball no matter where it bounced, returned it anyway for a clear winner well inside the sideline that incredulously was called "Out!"

Still, Smith overcame it all and prevailed in five sets to clinch the Cup. Too, he overcame the urge to punch the gamesman Tiriaic rather than shake his hand at the net afterwards. Instead, Smith coolly told him he no longer respected him, turned, and walked away.

Wayne Bryan—father of identical twins Mike and Bob, who even Smith and Lutz would not have wanted to see facing them across the doubles net—was the emcee for the evening and began his warm introduction of Smith with a roasting that belonged in a comedy club. Smith laughed so hard I half-expected his trademark blonde mustache to slip off his quivering lip.

But when the microphone was in Smith's hand, as with a tennis racket, he gave better than he got, displaying a wicked sense of humor and playfulness and grace.

Speaking of having a racket in his hand, when I showed Smith the old Pro Staff he smiled and instantly examined it. He explained how he personally nailed the butt cap secure and showed me where he twice tacked the old-school "Fairway" leather grip in place before tightly wrapping it on.

And then his right hand, a paw really for it is huge and strong, wrapped itself around the oversized 4-7/8 grip. All these years later, his fingers instinctively found their familiar grooves in the overlapping seams and he squeezed gently, caressingly almost, and waved the Wilson magic wand ever so slightly to better feel its heft and balance. From his contented smile, you could tell it was like he had been blissfully reunited with a dance partner from a long-ago Prom.

Then my boyhood hero returned to 2015 and, while I remained in 1970 a little longer, he signed the racket with a single double-tall script "S" next to "tan" which is above "mith."

And now you know the rest of the story, finally completed forty-five years later.

Forty-One

If You Can't Feed One Hundred...

IT was a recent evening, lovely even by Southern California standards, and after enjoying dinner at an Italian restaurant my daughter and I were walking to a theater. Along the way, predictably, we encountered a homeless man encamped on the sidewalk.

Also, predictably, he was begging for spare change. Predictably, too, my daughter instead offered him a take-out box containing half of a savory dinner, complete with plastic utensils she had thought to ask our waiter to include in anticipation of this scene.

"What is it?" the unkempt and unshaven man asked.

"Pasta and chicken," my daughter answered, adding with the enthusiasm of a waitress recommending the evening's special: "It's delicious!"

The man, wearing a knit cap despite the unseasonably warm evening, shook his head like a child who has been offered Brussels sprouts and waved his hands as though shooing away a pigeon. "Nah, I don't think I'd eat that," he said dismissively.

As we walked on, slightly stunned at the rejection, my daughter observed: "At least he was honest about it so we can give it to someone who will enjoy it."

Curmudgeonly, I said: "If it was a Big Mac you know he would have been thrilled."

Perhaps I was correct, but certainly my daughter was because on the very next block she succeeded in doing what Mother Teresa urged: "If you can't feed a hundred people, feed just one."

Truth is there are a hundred, and hundreds more, locally who need to be fed—and clothed and given a warm and dry place to sleep, especially on those nights far harsher than the one recalled above.

So I was dismayed by a newspaper opinion piece I recently read under the headline: "How to end homelessness? No extra services." The writer argued that the efforts of local faith leaders and their materialistic solutions to end homelessness will only worsen the problem, not help it.

Among the writer's contentions is that "the majority of the chronically homeless have substance abuse and/or mental illness issues they simply refuse to deal with responsibly."

But therein lies the Rubik's Cube: it is no *simple*

matter for anyone struggling with mental illness or substance abuse—even those with the financial means to afford the best help—to deal with these challenges responsibly.

Indeed, to complain, as the commentary did, "If they would just get clean and sober…" is to diminish not only the problem but the individuals, as though mental illness and addiction are a choice.

Compassion, on the other hand, is a choice. Treating the down-and-out with respect, not scorn, is a choice. Offering a helping hand is a choice. Choices we must make.

To be sure, help and services too often seem in vain. But if there were an easy fix, it would have happened already. I would rather have a citizenry that tries, and fails, to help the homeless than one that fails to try.

Just this week Pope Francis did something so small to help the poor that it is actually huge: a space off of St. Peter's Square has been transformed to offer homeless men and women shower facilities daily and free haircuts and shaves every Monday. The biggest offering: a little dignity.

Closer to home, Scott Harris is also trying to help the least among us in a way that often goes overlooked. His local firm, Mustang Marketing, just held its annual "Sleeping Bag Drive" and this year raised enough money to buy more than three hundred brand new sleeping bags for people in need.

"When it's all said and done," the warm-hearted Harris says, "no one should go to bed cold. We can make a difference."

Nor should anyone go to bed hungry. Walking back to our car after the show, my daughter and I again passed the homeless man who had wrinkled his nose at her pasta and chicken leftovers. He was eating a fast-food hamburger. Happily, someone else had made a small difference more to his liking.

Forty-Two

Super Bowl "Tin Man"

—

I think about Willie from time to time, which is saying something when you consider I met him only briefly twenty-two—or, in Roman Numerals, XXII—Januarys past.

I do not remember much from that Super Bowl XXVII in Pasadena I covered in 1993, but I have not forgotten Willie.

In truth, I see Willie still. I see him in town and downtown and at our beaches. I see him in parks and parking lots and lots of other places.

Willie was homeless.

I have long forgotten any down-and-out pass patterns run by Dallas Cowboys or Buffalo Bills receivers that distant Super Bowl Sunday, but the image of down-and-out Willie remains stored on my mental hard drive.

Troy Aikman was the game MVP and thus celebrated the Cowboys' one-sided victory by going to Disneyland; Willie probably celebrated by going to a soup kitchen. A restaurant meal was a Fantasyland for him.

I met Willie outside the Rose Bowl stadium a few hours before kickoff when he asked if he could have the soda can I was still drinking from. After I took a final gulp, Willie crushed it with a smooth foot stomp before flipping it into a grocery cart nearly brimming with other flattened cans and empty bottles.

We got to talking and I learned Willie's nickname was "Tin Man." While it would have been more accurate, L. Frank Baum never wrote about, and the band America never sang about, "*Aluminum* Man."

Certainly "Tin Man" looked as weathered as a rusty steel can and walked like his knees could use a few squirts from an oil can.

The Super Bowl is America's biggest tailgate party, but for Willie it was a big workday. The growing litter on the Rose Bowl grounds came into his focus like a field of blooming poppies outside Oz. Indeed, instead of earning the ten dollars or so he did on a typical day of scavenging, "Tin Man" figured he would collect a bounty of recyclables worth close to $100.

If he had ever been on it, "Tin Man" veered off the Yellow Brick Road years earlier. The cause might have been a lost job or catastrophic medical bills, alcoholism or drug addiction, mental illness or perhaps a combination of the aforementioned—I did not ask, he did not tell.

Just as Willie's shopping cart was overflowing with

empty cans, our world is overfilled with too many Tin Men and Tin Women, Tin Teens and Tin Children.

Even the great Oz would have been powerless in solving homelessness, but still we must try. I know this: there but for the grace of God any one of us could go.

The cold truth: 3.5 million people experience homelessness in the U.S. annually and more than 1.6 million of them are children. In California the figure for homeless kids is 226,000. To put that into local perspective where I live, there are 4,000 homeless schoolchildren in Ventura County alone, according to the Ventura County Office of Education.

By any measure homelessness is a huge problem. Countless people and agencies are fighting the good fight. But all of our combined efforts need to be redoubled. And redoubled again.

Different things can unlock a brighter future for a homeless person: food and shelter, of course, but also counseling; clean clothes for a job interview; access to showers in order to keep a job. I cannot help but wonder is some of these assistances could have changed the course of Willie's life.

Leaving the press tent after filing that long-ago Super Bowl column, I saw "Tin Man" still toiling. I went back inside and got him a couple hot dogs and a soda.

"Thanks, man," Willie said, his one-tooth-missing

smile flashing warmly on a chilly winter night. "You're all right."

Truth is, it wasn't much at all, but doing nothing is all wrong.

Forty-Three

Pooh Bear and Tears

WHEN my daughter was very young and in daycare, I would frequently pick her up and take her out on a lunch "date." We always had a wonderful time, but when I would drop her off again so I could go back to work, she always cried.

And cried and cried, so much so that her grandmotherly caregiver, Jeannie, eventually suggested it might be best to stop these noontime special excursions.

The next time I dropped Dallas off after a lunch outing, I tried something crazy and gave her one of her favorite stuffed animals to remind her of me, and our bedtime reading ritual, as she went down for her afternoon nap.

Winnie the Pooh worked like a charm. The tears stopped, nearly, and our dates continued happily.

Fast forward just over a dozen years. After hugging Dallas goodbye on move-in day her freshman year in college, I handed her a small stuffed Winnie the Pooh.

Through her tears emerged a smile, like a rainbow through a drizzle.

I really need not have worried, of course. Minutes after we left, Dallas' very first new college friend walked into her dorm room. This human Winnie the Pooh's name was Celine. She lived across the hallway and came bearing an extra Popsicle.

Instant friends, they became roommates the following three years, and lasting friends who, after graduation, visited each other around the globe from Los Angeles and San Francisco to London and Paris, the latter where Celine moved to pursue her dream career in fashion.

On a Monday morning, much too early to be anything except a wrong number or tragic news, Dallas phoned me. It was the latter, heartbreak like I have never heard in her voice: "Celine is dead, Daddy."

Celine was in India for a friend's wedding and while riding in a taxi was hit by a bus. Twenty-six is far too young to lose your life and twenty-seven is far too young to lose a best friend.

Talking to Dallas on the phone numerous times daily since—in truth, mostly listening to her because a parent is hopelessly impotent to help in any other way in such a tragic time—I have been reminded of those long ago nights reading to her about another friendship, from A.A. Milne's classic *Winnie the Pooh,* and specifically the passage where Christopher Robin tells Pooh Bear:

"If ever there is tomorrow when we're not together, there is something you must always remember. You are braver than you believe, stronger than you seem, and smarter than you think."

Celine, in a way, gave this same gift to Dallas, who recalls: "Freshman year of college, when I broke up with my first real boyfriend, I remember fleeing to her room, sobbing, and Celine hugged me as I cried.

"Another time, when I was feeling down on myself because 'no boys were ever going to like me, *ever!*' she played me the song 'Somebody's Baby' by Phantom Planet, saying it made her think of me because I was 'so awesome that guys probably just assume you're already taken.' I still smile and think of her when I hear that song. Celine saw the very best in me, even when I didn't see it in myself."

The last time my daughter saw Celine was before Dallas' birthday this past May. They caught up for brunch before Celine caught her flight back to Paris.

"I had a cold and I remember wondering whether I should cancel," Dallas recalls. "I didn't want to spread my germs to Celine, or to anyone else my path would cross on my commute into the city. But we were able to see each other so rarely that I thought, 'To hell with it, I'm going!' And I'm so grateful I did. We had a lovely visit, chatting in the sunshine over hot coffee and tea and scones, and before we hugged goodbye in the BART station I remembered to snap a photo."

One could not wish to see two happier faces in a final selfie together.

Here is what Christopher Robin also tells Pooh Bear: "But the most important thing is, even if we're apart... I'll always be with you."

He should have added, "Here, Pooh, have a Popsicle."

Forty-Four

What I Love Now

———

MY kids. Nick. Spring. Fall. Waffles. The concept of waffles. Bacon.

These are the first few things writer-filmmaker Nora Ephron listed in her short essay titled "What I Will Miss" in her most-recent book *I Remember Nothing And Other Reflections.*

A walk in the park. The idea of a walk in the park. The park. Shakespeare in the Park. The bed. Reading in bed.

It is a superb essay, like all of Ephron's writing, but when I read it—not in bed, for I am not an in-bed reader—I remember thinking it seemed out of place; she was too young; this was an essay for a future book.

Fireworks. Laughs. The view out the window. Twinkle lights. Butter. Dinner at home just the two of us. Dinner with friends. Dinner with friends in cities where none of us lives.

I had missed the clues that seem so obvious now: the essay "What I Won't Miss" (*Dry skin. E-mail. Funerals. Small print. E-mail. I know I already said it, but I want to emphasize it*.) on the two previous pages; and the Acknowledgements page that concluded, "And also, of course, my doctors."

Like the great writer she was, Ephron had told us without telling us. *Paris. Next year in Istanbul.* Pride and Prejudice. *The Christmas tree. Thanksgiving dinner. One for the table. The dogwood. Taking a bath. Coming over the bridge to Manhattan. Pie.*

She of course knew then what we know now. She was battling leukemia. A battle she lost on Tuesday, June 26, 2012, at age seventy-one.

Here is what I hope, that Nora Ephron wrote "What I Will Miss" long before she became ill—but under a different title, such as perhaps "What I Love Now." Such a list is something we should all write, right now, whatever our age, to help us more fully appreciate and enjoy these things today.

Here, off the top of my head, is my working draft of "What I Love Now"—I hope you will take some time to start your own. Here goes:

My kids. My wife. My extended family and great friends—and Murray, our boxer, who is both.

The beach. The ocean. *The Old Man and the Sea.*

The Ventura Pier. The Channel Islands. A Pacific sunset with a few clouds on the horizon that explode in flames of color.

Yosemite Falls. Niagara Falls. The fall colors.

Summer. Daylight saving time. Watching fireworks on the Fourth of July.

The smell of sunscreen, the smell in the air after a rain, the smell of Thanksgiving all afternoon long.

Fleetwood Mac. The Beatles. The Who. James Taylor.

Running along the beach, any beach, in a park, especially New York's Central Park, in the sun, in the rain, in a road race, and the adventures of running in a new place.

Once a Runner. The Adventures of Huckleberry Finn. To Kill a Mockingbird. Catcher in the Rye. Any really good read, and this definitely includes books by my gifted storyteller Venturan friends Ken McAlpine, Jeff McElroy, and Roger Thompson.

Newspapers.

A hot shower. A warm bed. A cold pint. (Not in that order.)

The last moments awake in bed after a long, full day. Even better, with the sound of rain on the roof.
The sound of Vin Scully on the radio.

Date nights. Van Gogh's *Starry Night*. A tiger painting, among others, by my son.

Chocolate-chip ice cream, chocolate-chip cookies, chocolate chips, not always in moderation.

Visiting my daughter and son, wherever they call home, and their daily texts, e-mails, phone calls, and trips *home*.

John Wooden's Pyramid of Success and my favorite Wooden-ism: "Make each day your masterpiece."

The simple grace and quiet strength of trees and rivers—and some people. People who have empathy and authenticity. Curious people who never stop learning.

The Internet, in moderation.

Finishing writing something that I feel is as good as I can do.

Movies, which for this list today seems fitting to pick three by Nora Ephron, even though I get them confused: *When Harry Met Sally*, *Sleepless In Seattle*, and *You've Got Mail*.

And yes, waffles over pancakes, definitely.

My kids. Lisa. I know I already said this, but I want to emphasize it.

Forty-Five

Jewell of a Friendship

———

"GIVING does not empty your hands," says my son, Greg, wise beyond his years. "It prepares them to be filled."

Too, giving prepares your heart to be filled. Caregivers Assisting The Elderly, which is celebrating its thirtieth anniversary in Ventura County, is proof of this.

A decade past, as a high school sophomore, my daughter became a volunteer for Caregivers' "Building Bridges" intergenerational program. Her heart was filled by the experience.

"After school and on weekends, groups of teenagers supervised by Caregiver adults visit the homes of senior citizens and help them with gardening, cleaning, and other household chores," Dallas notes. "But the most requested service is simply providing a few minutes of company."

Caregivers as friendship givers.

By coincidence, Jewell Butcher lived alone less than a mile away from Dallas.

It was no coincidence Jewell's house was freshly painted as bright yellow as a sunflower on the outside, and inside the blue of a cloudless summer sky. Jewell, then seventy-six, had recently survived a heart attack and when she returned home she wanted to be surrounded by cheerful colors.

"The obvious pleasure she found in our company filled my heart," Dallas recalls of her first Caregivers visit with Jewell. "She told us a little about herself, but mostly asked questions—about school, about our families, about our dreams."

Bidding goodbye, Jewell hugged Dallas and warmly said: "Please come back soon."

Dallas did. She dropped by "The Sunflower House" frequently. Jewell would make tea and the two would talk for hours on end.

"She was a natural storyteller who delighted in the smallest details," Dallas remembers. "I learned that as a young woman, Jewell and her mother moved to California from Missouri. She had lived in Ventura for more than half a century and I loved hearing what my hometown was once like."

Long before Caregivers assisted Jewell, she was the caregiver for her mother through a long terminal illness.

"Even when sharing a sad story," Dallas marvels, "Jewell would end it with a smile and say, 'I sure am lucky.

I've had such a blessed life.' She was an inspiration."

Around the time Dallas moved off to college, Jewell moved into an assisted living facility. They talked about the similarity of the new chapters in their lives: "I was making new friends in the dorms and going to parties on weekends; she was making new friends in the dining hall and going to bingo nights."

In Dallas's absence, her younger brother visited Jewell.

"She never married and had no children, but I like to think Greg and I became her surrogate grandchildren," Dallas says, adding happily: "Other Townehouse residents often assumed we were her grandkids and she always smiled and never corrected them."

Going out to lunch delighted Jewell, and Dallas laughingly remembers how her frail companion sprinkled Splenda on most everything—even syrupy pancakes and crepes.

But an even sweeter memory was the time Jewell asked Dallas and Greg to drive her to the store because she dearly wanted a disposable camera.

"We had to go *right away* in the middle of a visit," Dallas retells, smiling at the memory. "When we finally returned to her room, the urgency of her request became clear—she wanted to take a picture of the three of us to hang on her refrigerator."

"I miss you when you're away," Jewell told them.

"We miss you, too," they answered, sincerely.

When the photos were developed, Jewell mailed copies to Dallas and Greg. She also enclosed a snapshot of her wearing a sky-blue scarf Dallas knitted as a gift the previous Christmas.

"I love that photo," Dallas says. "I have it in a frame on my dresser. Jewell's smile was contagious—and still is."

Having one's heart filled eventually exacts a steep price: heartache. Three years ago this week, a brief illness claimed Jewell's life at age eighty-six.

"I was living in Indiana and as always sent my dear friend a card for Valentine's Day," Dallas shares. "Jewell died on February 12, but I like to think she received my card before she passed."

I like to think so, too. I know this: a friendship like theirs is a rare Jewell.

Forty-Six

Boys of Summer '75 Still

———

THE memory hadn't flashed across my mind's eye in three decades, yet here it was in sharp focus and brilliant Kodachrome color.

The year was 1975 and the yellow VW Bug was already old and the summer was hot and here is the thing I most remember all these years later: there was no way to turn off the heater in my friend Jim's car.

Even with the windows rolled down we simmered like astronauts inside an Apollo space capsule during re-entry with the heat shield glowing red-hot.

Jim and I traveled what seemed like a roundtrip-to-the-moon worth of miles in that sweltering VW capsule, going to junior tennis tournaments in other cities and to public courts around town. I was an incoming sophomore, back when the high school was just three grades, and a year away from my driver's license. Jim, a senior and teammate, was always happy to give me a lift.

You remember funny things, like this: getting ice

cream cones after a practice session and coming out to find Jim had locked the keys in the VW. We borrowed a coat hanger from the nearby dry cleaners and, as the ice cream melted, took turns trying to break in by threading the straightened wire between the top of the driver's window and rubber padding and then maneuvering the bent end to hook around the lock-unlock knob and pulling it up.

The next time it happened, which it did, we ate our ice cream first.

I cannot tell you what songs played on Jim's car radio that magic summer, but my guess is they included Creedence Clearwater Revival's "Lodi" and "Motherless Child" by Eric Clapton and "Blue Sky" by The Allman Brothers Band and Paul Simon's "Diamonds on the Soles" and "Can't You See" by The Marshall Tucker Band.

I say this because those were all on the play list by The James Broz. Band on a recent August night inside a Ventura Harbor café venue not much roomier than Jim's VW Bug, although thankfully, much cooler.

The James Broz. Band is not brothers but rather a father and son—Jim and James Wolff. Actually, Jim goes by J.D. now, which keeps tripping me up.

Until last weekend, I believe I had seen Jim—I mean, J.D.—only twice in the past quarter-century. Both times he was playing drums in bands at large charity gatherings so we were unable to catch up.

One of the great things about social media is its ability to reconnect lost friends. Through Facebook, I had learned about the two-man James Gang's small gig and showed up. I am so glad I did.

J.D. is as talented with guitar strings as he was with gut strings in a tennis racket, and his son is no less musically gifted. Between songs J.D. kindly gave me a public shout-out, although in the intimate gathering shouting was not required.

"I want to thank my ol' friend Greg for coming out," Jim said, using my given name before quickly adding: "I mean, Woody."

There was no need for the correction—Jim is grandfathered in to call me Greg.

Between sets we got to visit and it was like a time portal. Jim's laugh is as unchanged as his fingerprints and I was reminded of a quote by the writer E.B. White: "I've never been able to shed the mental image I have of myself —a lad of about nineteen."

For me, make that about fifteen.

Now in our fifties, but both of us dressed like teens in jeans and flip-flops, Jim and I learned both of our sons have been to Africa on humanitarian sojourns and we each have a remarkable daughter and an amazing wife. I wanted to know more about his music; he wanted to talk about my new memoir *Wooden & Me*.

We promised to get together, and soon, and we have.

Moments earlier, Jim had sung Bob Dylan's "My Back Pages" and I thought about those lyrics and the turning of our own pages. Ah, we were so much younger then in that VW sauna, but that is all right because it takes a long time to grow an old friend.

Forty-Seven

A Hart-Warming Reunion

TENNESSEE Williams was spot-on when he observed, "Time doesn't take away from friendship, nor does separation."

Rarely has this been more clear personally than earlier this week, when I met up with a boyhood friend I had not seen in a dozen years, if not more. Before that, it had been nearly as long again between reunions.

Prior to these long lapses, however, during our "Wonder Years," Jimmy Hart and I were thick as thieves, or scamps, or Tom and Huck. He was, in fact, my first new friend upon moving to Ventura from Ohio at age twelve.

Jimmy, four months my junior, wasn't my friend so much as my "cousin" of which I have nary a single biological one. Had he lived in Ventura, or I in Pasadena, we would have instead been "brothers."

We first met because Jimmy's aunt and uncle were my godparents. Each summer he stayed two weeks at their Solimar (translation: "sun and sea") Beach home and upon arriving here in 1972, I joined him. It became a yearly rendezvous through our teens.

Those beach days and nights were boyhood bliss. We stayed up late shooting pool and watching TV, slept in long, then spent the remaining sunlight in the waves and exploring tidal pools, looking for seashells and ocean glass, playing basketball and, of course, talking about girls.

Too, I would annually stay a week with Jimmy and his mom—his father died when Jimmy was four and his only sibling, a sister, was ten years older and already out of the house—in Pasadena. Summer at the beach is an idyllic playground that is hard to equal, but these city vacations came close.

Jimmy was a California beach boy straight from Central Casting, with a toothpaste-ad smile, longish platinum hair, and a deep tan the color of an old penny. But his most striking feature, it always seemed to me, was his laugh.

Even at age twelve, his laugh sounded like it came from an old man with emphysema—imagine Billy Crystal doing an out-of-breath character in a Brooklyn deli. Better yet, recall the wonderful hearty snicker of Muttley, the Hanna-Barbera cartoon dog. That was Jimmy's Hart-y laugh and he used it readily.

Separation of seventy miles—Jimmy still lives near Pasadena—is no excuse for the years of disconnection we allowed to pass.

Our last time together was when we saw John Wooden give a talk at the historic Pasadena Civic Center. Jimmy and I shared many similarities growing up and near top of the list was our idolization of the Wizard of Westwood. Indeed, we both went to Coach Wooden's summer basketball camp and memorized every block in the Pyramid of Success.

Too bad we neglected Wooden's preaching to "make friendship a fine art"—at least with each other. Annually our Christmas cards echoed sentiments to rekindle our friendship in the New Year, but we kept failing to keep the promise.

Taking the "Initiative"—a block in Wooden's Pyramid—Jimmy's 2014 holiday card included wishes of "Peace, Love & Joy" and a specific date in January to meet. When I walked into Brendan's Irish Pub & Restaurant in Agoura Hills, a midway drive for both of us, the sight of my old friend was a time machine making me young again.

Our fifteen-year separation might as well have been five minutes. We picked up as if we had just been in the middle of a conversation before one of us left to go to the bathroom, the latter happening a number of times on this evening, causing Jimmy to joke, "I guess we are in our fifties and not teenagers anymore."

An anticipated hour visit lasted nearly four as we

reminisced and caught up on wives and kids, work and play, and raised our glasses to the shared loved ones we have lost—his cousin and my dear big "sister" Karen; his aunt and my godmother; his mom and my mom.

Bidding goodbye, Jimmy and I made plans for another hello very soon, and these words of Henry Wadsworth Longfellow came to mind: "Ah, how good it feels! The hand of an old friend."

And the warm hug and Hart-y laugh, too.

Forty-Eight

An Act of Grace

KaBOOM! KaBOOM! KaBOOM!

The racket sounded like a judge frantically trying to restore order in his courtroom.

Instead of a gavel, however, this ruckus was the pounding of eleven small, wooden mallets upon two tabletops. Specifically, two dining tables covered with butcher paper taped down at the corners.

And the butcher paper was covered with mountainous piles of *Callinectes sapidus:* Maryland Blue Crabs, fresh from the Chesapeake Bay.

There are a handful of meals over one's lifetime that stand out above all others and this dinner last summer in Falls Church, Virginia, makes my honor roll. Beyond the delicious food, this was due to the fine company. Oh, and the messy fun that made me feel like a kindergartener in need of an art smock.

Indeed, when I arrived my hosts—the aptly named Grace, and her husband Duane—apologized for not warning me to wear an old shirt.

Since I was a blue crab virgin, Grace's father, Ray, gave me a cracking tutorial. He began by showing me how to locate the crab's apron—a male's looks like the nearby Washington Monument while the female's resembles the Capitol dome—and then breaking it off.

Ray lost me somewhere between removing the top shell and cleaning the gills, but I latched onto the most important step: Pound the crab with the mallet, and with gusto, and then pick out and eat the sweet meat, again with gusto.

What I lacked in skill, I made up for with enthusiasm. Half-a-dozen crabs into the feast, I needed a clean shirt; after a dozen, a shower. Still, I kept going.

This was Thanksgiving in August. Instead of an oversized turkey, Grace served up a full bushel of steaming blue crabs seasoned by the gods. Half as many would have been a challenge to finish, but the eleven of us did our mighty messy best.

"You learn a lot about someone when you share a meal together," Anthony Bourdain, chef and TV personality, has said.

I learned that Ray was in the CIA during the Cold War and I learned much of Grace's charm comes from her mother, Anne.

I learned that in just about any endeavor, Duane

would be my top draft pick. A Southern California beach boy, he was a discus thrower on scholarship in college and now does triathlons; he is a masterful furniture maker and also built entirely by himself their large, gorgeous home that merits being featured in *Better Homes and Gardens*.

Too, he is an involved dad of two terrific teenage sons; a wonderful storyteller; modest as a monk; and generous beyond belief.

Actually, the last thing I already knew about Duane and Grace. You see, when my son accepted a ten-week summer internship in Washington, D.C., with KaBOOM!, a national non-profit dedicated to promoting active play for kids, he needed a place to stay.

I have a dear Venturan friend who grew up in Virginia and I asked him for recommendations where to look for potential housing. Ken in turn emailed a childhood friend for suggestions; Grace instantly phoned back saying they would happily take in the stranger.

"Who does that?" my wife said in joyous wonderment, her sleepless nights of worrying where our son would stay now cured.

Grace, Duane, Robbie and Scott, and charismatic collie-mix Hobie, made Greg feel so welcome that when I showed up for the crab feast only I was a visitor. Instead of a lonely rented room, Greg came home each night to a family. If he was running late, they held dinner. If he needed a ride, they drove him or gave him the car keys. When they went to parties and barbecues, Greg was included. Their kindness did not end when Greg's internship did—now working in New York City, he joined them this past Thanksgiving.

"We cannot tell the precise moment when friendship is formed," Ray Bradbury wrote. "As in filling a vessel drop by drop, there is at last a drop which makes it run over; so in a series of kindnesses there is at last one which makes the heart run over."

Grace and Duane proved Bradbury wrong, for they filled the vessel to overflowing even more quickly than eleven hungry souls emptied a bushel of delicious Maryland Blue Crabs.

Forty-Nine

My Two Cents on Tips

———

HELLO and welcome to today's essay. When you are done reading, please drop a tip in the mail.

This is what the world is coming to, it seems. Asking for tips.

Tip jars. Tip glasses. Tip bowls, boxes and buckets. I have even seen a tip abalone shell. You see them everywhere. In cafes, coffee houses and bagel shops. In burrito huts, pizza parlors, burger joints. Doughnut shops, ice cream shops, sandwich shops.

I half-expect my bank teller to put out a tip jar soon.

"Tips!"

"Tips, Please!"

"Leave your change, will ya!"

Actually, I have not seen the latter sign on a jar or conch shell—yet. But I did see a humorous threat in the pick-up window of a gourmet food truck: "Every Time You Don't Tip A Child Gets A Mullet Haircut."

Yes, as Bob Dylan sang, times are a-changin'.

Rather, these are "Got any loose change?" times.

At first blush, these solicitations can leave a customer cold. I mean, why should you tip the barista who made your double-mocha-skinny-latte? Or the cashier who rings up the take-out order you are picking up? Isn't that their job?

Well, yes. But is it not a waitresses/waiter's job to take your order, serve your food and clear the table? Sure it is, yet we think nothing of leaving them a tip.

Actually, sometimes we think *a lot* about it—as in trying to mentally calculate percentages to know how much to tip. But I digress.

The point is this: it is expected that we leave tips in sit-down restaurants because the waitstaff depends on "gratuities" to bring their pay at least up to minimum wage.

Personally, I wish all restaurant owners would just raise their menu prices twenty percent and pass one hundred percent of this bump along to workers and save us the math-induced migraine.

The thing is, if anyone could use a booster shot for anemic wages more than waitresses and busboys it is fast-food hamburger helpers and teenagers scooping ice cream.

And while fifteen or eighteen or twenty-plus percent of a nice restaurant bill can be a tidy sum, a similar tip on a take-away bagel breakfast or pizza lunch deal is certainly not going to make you fall shy on your next car payment.

And yet how often do we ignore the tip jar/glass/bowl/box/bucket/abalone shell? Sometimes, if you are at all like me, your intentions are good but the paltry change you receive back from the cashier seems like an insult to drop in the tip jar.

This isn't a valid excuse because folding money is what we really should drop in. A dollar, or two, still often falls short of a fifteen-percent tip.

You will be surprised how grateful the person behind the counter will be for a two-buck tip. Drop an Abraham Lincoln, or a generous Alexander Hamilton, in the jar/glass/bowl/box/bucket/abalone shell and you will almost see cartwheels of gratitude.

Indeed, I now enthusiastically embrace tip jars because the workers truly make it feel like you have given a "gratuity" instead of giving something expected.

In fact, I am disappointed when there isn't a tip jar. This was especially the case when my recent take-out tab was nine cents over an even-dollar amount and I had no dime or any change. Nine cents was too much to take from the spare-penny dish, so I was doomed to getting back a pocketful of loose change.

Then my luck *changed*. The young man behind the counter gave me one of my dollar bills back, smiled, reached into his pocket and dropped his own dime into the register. With no tip jar, beyond a warm thank you the only gratuity I could give was to sing his praises to the manager.

And if you really want a philanthropic feeling for very little cost, buy an extra box of Girl Scout cookies and give it back to the salesgirl Scouts as a snack or tip a kid running a lemonade stand. I recently stopped to buy a $1 glass from two cute kids.

Their glee made it the best five bucks I can remember spending in a long time when I put the change of four singles in—what else?—their decorated tip jar.

Fifty

Overrated and Underrated

———

BEFORE seeing the summer action movie *Man of Steel*, I figured it had to be underrated with a published review of 1.5 out of 4 stars. After seeing it, however, 1.5 stars made it overrated.

Speaking of "Superman," Dwight Howard has been overrated his entire NBA career.

Adam West remains underrated as Batman.

Americans gave Congress a fifteen-percent approval rating in the most recent Gallup poll. In other words, Congress remains overrated.

Teachers are underrated and CEOs are overrated.

Twinkies were slightly underrated until they recently became extinct and were suddenly wildly overrated. Now Twinkies are back, at a slimmed-down 135 calories per cake instead of 150 calories, and their rating has rightly shrunk again.

Farmers markets are underrated.

Donald Trump may be the most overrated person

on earth. His hair cannot possibly be underrated.

Watermelon is overrated and bananas are underrated.

Strawberries in wintertime cannot be overrated.

The dangers firefighters and police face are underrated by most of us.

In-N-Out Burger is overrated by its faithful (guilty as charged) but underrated by everyone else who favors any other hamburger-fries-and-shakes fast-food chain.

The U.S. Postal Service is underrated.

Handwritten letters and cards and notes cannot be overrated.

Post-it Notes are underrated.

Everything about Florida is overrated, including, it pains me to say, Disney World.

Florida's juries, courts and judges cannot be underrated.

The iPhone is overrated as a phone, but underrated as a computer (as are all smartphones) when you consider these hand-held devices are said to be thousands of times faster and more powerful than the Apollo guidance system that landed men on the moon.

Everything about Apollo 11 is underrated.

Newspapers are underrated.

The value of having music and art education in our schools is underrated.

Prosecutors in high-profile murder cases tend to come out looking overrated after the verdict.

The importance of a jury selection cannot be overrated.

Butterflies and birds are underrated.

Having a good mechanic, plumber or handyman is underrated.

The long lines and hassles of airport security screening is overrated while the speed and relative ease—and general affordability—of traveling anywhere in the United States in a few hours is underrated.

Comfortable shoes are underrated until you are wearing vises on your feet.

Before one sees the Grand Canyon in person it cannot help but be overrated; standing on its rim, however, it is impossible to overrate its awe-inspiring grandeur and breathtaking beauty.

Yosemite Valley is probably underrated.

The Channel Islands are definitely underrated.

Taking hundreds of pictures and hours of video on vacation is overrated, even at the Grand Canyon, Channel Islands and Yosemite Valley.

Twitter is overrated.

Facebook is overrated… until you locate a long-lost friend or make some new ones you never would have otherwise.

Novacaine cannot be overrated if you are sitting in a dentist's chair getting a filling.

Local microbrews and wines are underrated.

Dogs are underrated even by people who overrate everything.

Even if you try to fully appreciate it, good health is underrated until you are ill or injured.

Teenagers overrate the calamity of having a few pimples.

Older people overrate the calamity a few gray hairs.

Local charities that humbly do tremendous work are underrated.

The "good ol' days" are overrated and today's youth are too often underrated by those who were youths back in the "good ol' days."

John Steinbeck's charming novel *Sweet Thursday* is underrated.

The Great Gatsby* is overrated. (* the movie, not the book)

To Kill A Mockingbird* is underrated (* movie and book)

Intelligence is often overrated but the importance of education is underrated.

Common sense is underrated.

Public libraries are underrated.

A good friendship cannot be overrated.

A friendly smile is underrated by the person sharing it with someone else.

Pizza is underrated. Period. Chocolate, too. Period.

Fifty-One

Hangerphobia

HOW many times has your mother, or wife or significant other, asked (pronounced "told") you, "Will you please hang up your clothes!"?

Personally, I lost count at about six—age six, that is.

Had I a quarter for every time I have heard that exasperated complaint, I could hire a butler to pick up after me.

To be honest, I am not all that bad at putting clothes away in dresser drawers.

And I am flat-out excellent at putting my clothes away on chairs. I can drape, layer and stockpile enough clothes for a week on a single chair and another week's worth on the seat and handlebars of an exercise bike. A circus performer spinning plates on sticks should have such a honed gift of balance.

But I have yet to master the art of using clothes hangers. I have not checked my symptoms on Web M.D. but I think I might be afflicted with "hangerphobia" or perhaps even "hangerexia nervosa."

Males are especially susceptible to both Oscar Madison-like maladies, although females are not immune. Teenage girls are proof of this; many are less frightened of spiders and snakes than handling hangers.

Let's face it, hangers can be very scary lurking in dark closets, hanging like one-legged bats with wings spread before attacking unsuspecting hands. Moreover, they often strike in pairs, groups and bunches.

Unlike socks that mysteriously disappear in the dryer, hangers, like rabbits, seemingly multiply overnight. Two explanations for this phenomenon are that hangers are reincarnated lost socks or perhaps hangers simply have no natural predators to thin the herd.

Well, they now have one—me!

Just once I would like to reach into my bedroom closet and grab a single hanger and pull it out without thirteen cousin hangers clamping onto my wrist like a school of hungry piranha.

Hangers apparently thought Benjamin Franklin was talking about them when he said, "We must all hang together, or assuredly we shall all hang separately."

Separating the wire pretzels, which always seem in the midst of a spirited game of Twister, is no simple task. Rubik's Cube is far easier to solve. Nerves of steel alone will not suffice. Patience and reason are all but useless.

A short temper, however, helps. Brute force is what hangers most respect. Frantic, angry shaking is the most effective method for separating clustered hangers.

After you finish playing fifty-two-hanger pickup, you must select the right hanger for the specific job. This is no small task for the variety of hanger designs is matched only by the curses they invoke.

Heavy and sturdy. Thin and frail. Metal, wood, plastic and composites of the three. Some swivel, some don't. But all raise one's blood pressure, especially the thief-proof hotel hangers.

Thin wire hangers are ill-suited for anything, sans perhaps T-shirts—and who hangs up a T-shirt? Drape a pair of jeans on one of these wimps and the sucker will bend and sag in the middle.

However, if you have locked your keys in the car, thin is your best choice for breaking in.

Plastic hangers are fine for most things except men's jeans, but are also more expensive and, in my experience, prone to being hogged by one's wife.

Chin-up bar gauged metal hangers rate Five Stars for everyday use. In fact, three out of four dry cleaners recommend these.

Tailors, on the other hand, endorse the use of wooden hangers for sport coats and dress pants.

Another choice to prevent leaving a crease across

pant legs is a hanger with a cardboard tube along the bottom. Unfortunately, the cardboard invariably bends or detaches, causing the pants to fall to the floor and get numerous creases.

Indeed, I find these hangers, actually *all* hangers, annoying—even more so than being asked (told), "Will you please hang up your clothes!"

My advice is to avoid these fragile hangers and skip the problem altogether by tossing your clothes directly onto the floor yourself.

Fifty-Two

Lessons From Louie

GENERALLY, I cannot recall what I had for lunch the previous day. Certainly if you ask me about three days past I will draw a blank. Yet I can tell you that the daily special in a Hollywood café on a sunny July afternoon fifteen years ago was meatloaf.

I remember this not because I ordered it, but because my lunch companion did—only to have the waitress return from the kitchen with news they were out of gravy. She asked Louie Zamperini what he would like to order instead.

My dessert that day was spending the rest of the afternoon with the legendary 1936 Olympic runner and World War II hero, listening to his life story while looking through couch cushion-sized scrapbooks.

Zamperini's death arrived on July 2, 2014 after he battled pneumonia for forty days. That may well be a world record for a ninety-seven-year-old to hold off pneumonia, but Louie always had the mettle for long, tough battles.

After his B-24 Liberator was shot down on May 27, 1943, Air Force Captain Louis Zamperini (and one crew member; a third crewmate died early on) drifted nearly two-thousand miles in the South Pacific, surviving for forty-seven days while fighting hunger, fighting thirst, fighting sharks.

"Two big sharks tried to jump in the raft and take us out," Zamperini—then eighty-three and so fit he still regularly hiked, skied and skateboarded—told me. After a sip of iced tea he added: "We went seven days without water. That was brutal."

Nourished only by rainwater, a few fish and sea birds, and two small sharks, the five-foot-nine Zamperini weighed a deathly sixty-seven pounds—eighty pounds below his racing weight—when a Japanese patrol boat picked him up.

Then the brutality turned truly hellish. For good reason Louie titled his autobiography *Devil at My Heels*.

And for good reason Laura Hillenbrand's bestselling biography of Zamperini is titled *Unbroken*. Even two and half years in a POW slave camp could not break him.

Certainly Japanese Army Sergeant Matsuhiro Watanabe tried to break Zamperini. "The Bird," as the prisoners called this devil incarnate, beat him daily. Beat him bloody. And, during one savage streak, used a belt buckle to beat Louie into unconsciousness fourteen days in a row.

For these reasons I called Zamperini "The Toughest Miler Ever" in my column after interviewing him.

Here is how great a miler Zamperini was: his national prep record set at Torrance High stood for a full twenty years. He was a back-to-back NCAA champion at USC and his 1939 national collegiate record (four minutes, eight seconds) stood for fifteen years.

Zamperini's greatest running victory, however, came off the cinder track.

"Absolutely, my athletic background saved my life," he told me. "I kept thinking about my athletic training when I was competing against the elements, against the enemy, against hunger and thirst. In athletics, you learn to find ways to increase your effort. In athletics you don't quit —ever!"

Zamperini shared other life lessons with me, like: "Faith is more important than courage."

And this: "I forgave The Bird." Only by doing so, he explained, did he finally escape his own post-war emotional prison.

And now there is a lesson in his death, too: that a single flower for the living is better than bouquets on a grave.

While it is wonderful *Unbroken* became a bestseller,

it is sad a movie of Zamperini's heroic life finally reached the silver screen five months after his death.

How much sweeter had the film been made in the 1950s (Tony Curtis wanted the role) or in the late 1990s (Nicolas Cage was interested) when Zamperini could have enjoyed it.

Similarly, how sorrowful that the Tournament of Roses waited until 2015 to honor Zamperini as its Grand Marshal. Did parade organizers think he would live forever? Why wait until he was ninety-seven? Was he any less worthy of the honor at eighty-seven or sixty-seven?

Back to lunch. I fondly remember Louie's answer when the waitress told him there was no gravy.

No matter. Not after what he had endured. The Toughest Miler Ever smiled and ordered the meatloaf anyway.

Fifty-Three

"Special" Olympians

——

DURING a quarter century as a sports columnist, I had the great fortune to cover Super Bowls, World Series, NBA Finals, Grand Slam golf tournaments and heavyweight title bouts, but when it comes to goose bumps and inspiration, no event can top the Olympics.

The Special Olympics, specifically.

Baron Pierre de Coubertin, father of the modern Olympics, famously said: "The important thing in the Olympic Games is not to win, but to take part. The important thing in life is not the triumph, but the struggle. The essential thing is not to have conquered, but to have fought well."

Each of the many times I have attended a Special Olympics sporting event, I have witnessed a collection of athletes who personify de Coubertin's maxim to the fullest. While their triumphs are few, their struggles are great. They did not all conquer, but they all fought well, each and every courageous one of them.

While I have yet to witness a world record fall at a Special Olympic meet, some of the competitors have fallen. But only those who are blessed enough to be able to stand in the first place.

Something else usually falls: tears of spectators, designated huggers and even meet officials who watch the heroic efforts put forth by these truly *Special* Olympians.

Challenged by intellectual or/and physical disabilities, these participants do not stand a prayer of making it to the International Olympic Games. Heavens, it is only through prayer that many of these kids and adults manage to get out of bed each morning, let alone compete athletically.

To be sure, the accomplishments by these competitors are no less golden than those of Olympic champions. More golden, perhaps. More inspirational, for certain.

An Olympic marathon champion can cover 26.2 miles in just over two hours. Big deal. Surely it takes more heart, more grit, more determination to stagger fifty meters in barely less time than it takes to boil a three-minute egg when you do so on two legs that wobble like a newborn colt taking its first steps.

In my collage of indelible press-box memories with such mental snapshots as Joe Montana leading a game-winning drive, Magic Johnson leading a fast break, and

Jack Nicklaus charging on the back nine, was seeing a twelve-year-old girl stumble and scrape both her knobby knees.

What really put a lump the size of an Oxnard strawberry in my throat was not the young girl's blood, but rather her guts. She got up, with assistance, and finished what for her was a 100-meter *marathon* to roaring cheers and standing applause worthy of Montana, Magic, or Jack at their finest.

To quote the ancient Greek hero Pheidippides: "Rejoice. Victory is ours." Victory was hers. For her gallant effort she received a modest medallion and I guarantee you Joan Benoit Samuelson does not covet her Olympic marathon gold medal half so dearly.

To a man and boy, woman and girl, Special Olympians epitomize the organization's lofty motto: "Let me win, but if I cannot win let me be brave in the attempt."

For a person partially paralyzed, competing in the beanbag *drop* or being pushed in a wheelchair to the finish line in the 50-meter slalom—yes, at local meets there are such events—requires the same bravery as the shot put or 400-meter dash.

The Special Olympics now offers opportunity to more than four million participants, but its impact is best measured individually. For example, my boyhood friend Charlie's life was enriched greatly, even into adulthood, through his involvement in Special Olympics swim meets.

Too, there is the ripple effect. My friend, Gary, was inspired to become a Special Needs physical therapist because of his Special Olympian kid brother who he calls his hero.

If you ever have an opportunity to attend a Special Olympics meet, I implore you to do so. From bowling, badminton, and basketball to swimming, powerlifting, and the half-marathon, their speed, strength, and coordination will blow you away.

More than that, their spirit and bravery will.

Fifty-Four

Courageous Casey

———

AFTER you finish reading this first paragraph, take a timeout. Get up from your chair and walk across the room… with your eyes closed.

Okay, go ahead now. Try not to stub your toe or break a lamp—or arm.

Are you back? Good. How far did you make it before you peeked? Two steps? Ten?

Now imagine walking six *miles* with your eyes shut tight. Six miles, not indoors across your carpeted family room, but rather outdoors over a rocky hiking trail. Six rugged miles, including fording a stream eight times, every step of the way blindfolded.

If you were blind, would you dare to go on such a hike?

My dear friend Casey Cook has.

He has also blindly conquered a triathlon consisting of a one-mile ocean swim (with kayaker keeping him on line), fifty-six-mile bike ride (on a tandem) and thirteen-mile run (with a guide).

Too, Casey has gone water skiing, body surfing and whitewater rafting. On one rafting trip he purposely dived overboard in order to better experience the water's rush. His shocked companions and river guide were all moved to tears by his courage.

The national ARETE Awards, which aim to celebrate the ancient Greek's ideal of "Courage in Sports," for good reason honored Casey in 1998. Previous honorees include Muhammad Ali and Arthur Ashe. Of course they never had to compete blindfolded.

Casey Terrence Cook has been blind since age nine when a genetic disorder called Voigte-Carnegie Syndrome robbed him of his eyesight—and two years later cruelly stole his hearing as well. One thing Voigte-Carnegie Syndrome was never able to take away was Casey's courage.

"I wasn't going to let it ruin my life," Casey, now forty-one years old, says. True to his word he hasn't.

Blind and deaf, Casey was a varsity swimmer, cross country runner and wrestler (with a 14-4 record) at Rio Mesa High in Oxnard, California.

Blessedly, in 1992 at age eighteen, the miracles of modern medicine released Casey from his prison of silence thanks to a cochlear implant. The receptor and twenty-two thin wires were surgically implanted above his right ear and can translate sound into electrical signals to be "heard" by his brain.

He has since heard a lot of cheering. This remarkable six-foot-two, 195-pound athlete has won medals at the Paralympics, the U.S. Association of Blind Athletes Road Nationals and the World Cycling Championships for the Disabled.

This remarkable person has also earned a degree in rehabilitation counseling at Cal State Los Angeles and for the past sixteen years has worked for the Department of Rehabilitation's Blind Field Services in Los Angeles. Casey, who has been married for ten years, gives new—and positive—meaning to the phrase "the blind leading the blind" by assisting the sightless in getting jobs or keeping the jobs they already have.

"I don't think I'm anything special," says Casey, sincerely but wrongly. "I'm not a role model."

He is wrong on both counts. He is a special role model. Indeed, when I am faced with what I consider to be a daunting challenge I often think back to the first time Casey asked me to be his running guide while training for a 10K road race we also ran in tandem. To signal me to go faster, Casey—who lightly holds onto my left elbow with his right hand as we run in tandem—would softly push my arm forward.

Near the end of our training run, I felt Casey

squeeze my elbow so I picked up the pace.

He squeezed tighter still, so I went a little faster still; tighter again, faster again.

Only then did I look over and notice that Casey was grimacing and grabbing for his left hamstring. I had misinterpreted his signal—he did not want me to speed up, but instead was gripping me tighter for balance.

But there was no misinterpreting his courage. He hadn't stopped running despite a painful pulled muscle. It is the perfect metaphor for the way Casey lives his life: nothing stops him.

"I'm used to people thinking I can't do something. I like to prove them wrong," says Casey, adding profoundly: "I wish I could open their eyes to what they can do instead of being afraid to experience life."

Fifty-Five

Frank-ly Inspiring

———

CHANCES are good that, just five days into January, you have already broken some of your New Year's resolutions. Maybe all of them. Or perhaps you do not believe in resolutions to start a new year.

Early two Januarys past—if it was not the first day it was surely the first week—I saw a heavy-set middle-aged man jogging near my neighborhood. After a couple more sightings, I assumed his New Year's resolution was to lose weight, gain health.

If this was his resolution for the new year, he beat the odds by having the rare resolve to not quit. Indeed, I continued to see him jogging frequently and while I did not notice it daily, or even weekly, over the course of the changing seasons it became obvious his pace was quickening, his breathing becoming less labored.

And his T-shirt and shorts grew baggier.

Each encounter with The Jogging Man has lifted my spirits for two reasons: I am happy for him and he makes me think of my dear friend Frank who lives seventy miles away.

Last March, Frank turned fifty. Over the previous two decades his weight soared like a dot-com stock in the late 1990s; it peaked at 311 pounds on January 5, 2014.

Instead of on the customary January 1, Frank made his New Year's resolution five days later. He joined a gym, hired a certified personal trainer to work with him three times a week, and equally importantly hired a nutritionist who has proved to be equal parts counselor, therapist, and psychologist as well.

Asked the other evening what his nutritionist has taught him, Frank's answer is surprising. He does not talk about fats, carbohydrates and protein; about counting calories or cutting out this or eating that.

Here is Frank's initial answer: tears. For a long moment he is at a complete loss for words, a rare occurrence for this gregarious husband and dad. Eventually he wipes his eyes, gathers his composure, and confides: "I learned it wasn't about food. I was unhappy."

The stress of running a window business when foreclosed homes were being boarded up at a frightening pace certainly played a role in his shuttered joy. This in turn led to late-night binges on pizza and ice cream—"The same problem carbs everyone has," he allows—that helped stoke his expanding waistline.

Frank's eyes again well up when speaking about his personal trainer who has motivated him so greatly that over the past year (as I write this essay) Frank has done a cardio workout every single day without fail. Many days, twice.

At the beginning his cardio workout was walking slowly, and briefly, on a flat treadmill. Gradually the distance increased and the spinning belt sped up and the incline grew steeper.

And gradually, like The Jogging Man I see in my neighborhood, Frank shrank. Drastically, like a wool shirt in a clothes dryer set to "Hot," until today he comes into focus like a winning contestant on "The Biggest Loser" reality TV show.

Here is the remarkable reality: at his last weigh-in on December 31, Frank weighed…

… 196!

He has lost 115 pounds. Moreover, he has added muscle—and self-esteem, confidence, happiness.

Before, Frank literally could not see his shoes to tie them; now, he looks downright athletic in sneakers. Before, he could not do a single pushup; now, he cranks out eight sets of twenty-five daily, plus two hundred sit-ups. His face looks ten years younger, at least.

His wife bought him new jeans the other day, beaming as she handed him the size-36s. Frank smiled at an even higher wattage when he tried them on and had to tell her to return them for 34s, a size he last wore in college.

"What clicked?" I asked Frank, who the past decade had experienced a litany of health problems related to his weight. "What finally made you do something?"

Again the answer is tears. The previous Christmas, Frank's mom confronted him and tearfully said she did not want to bury him.

This Christmas the son gave his mom the best present she could have wished for. Again she cried. This time happily. Mother's Day in December.

Fifty-Six

Mother's Day

A century ago in 1914, President Woodrow Wilson proclaimed the second Sunday in May as a national holiday in honor of mothers, although perhaps the biggest beneficiaries were the three-year-old Hall Brothers greeting card company (which would later change its name to Hallmark) and the four-year-old Florists' Telegraph Delivery Association (better known as FTD) which was the country's first flowers-by-mail service.

To be sure, cards, flowers, and Mother's Day go together like hot fudge, nuts, and ice cream.

So what if you forgot your mom's birthday (although she would never, ever forget yours); worried her half-to-death by missing curfew without calling or texting; haven't taken the trash out since the first iPhone came out; or as an adult only visit on holidays or when you cannot find a babysitter for the grandkids. Just give mom a bouquet of flowers—even a handful of dandelions will do —and all of the above will be forgiven.

Wives, fiancés, and girlfriends are of course rarely so forgiving. In fact, oftentimes flowers actually make them suspicious because they figure such a random act of husband/boyfriend kindness may be motivated by guilt. "What did you do?" they wonder.

Such is not the case with dear ol' mom—she won't even get upset with you for using the word "old" no matter how young she is. Just as a rose is a rose is a rose, so too is a son always a son and a daughter always a daughter. Love may be blind, but a mother's love cannot even read Braille. It is a good bet even Charlie Sheen's mother loves him.

While roles have changed greatly over the past decade or two, the lion's share of child rearing still falls upon the lionesses. Statistics show that it continues to be most often moms who change the diapers and get up in the middle of the night for feedings… arrange play dates and pediatrician appointments… care for chicken pox and wash socks… drive the family taxi and attend every teacher conference and never miss a school play and on and on.

The very least moms deserve in return is an annual "My Special Mom" FTD bouquet and sappy Hallmark card. And, if you are grown and out of the house, also a visit or at least a telephone call—even a simple "luv u Ma" text message will likely make her tear up.

This Mother's Day for the twenty-third year in a row I will not have someone to give a card to. Or, more importantly, give a hug to. Instead, I will recall warm memories of my mom—and smile when the phone rings for my wife with a call from our daughter in the Bay Area and again from our son in New York City.

I know it will be hard on my wife not to have them home, though not nearly as difficult as when she came home after their births while they remained in the hospital: the daughter for nearly three months after being born prematurely, and the son for three days with jaundice.

In the twenty-eight and twenty-six years since, my wife has learned much about motherhood. Recently, a friend who has younger children asked her: "When do we finally stop worrying about our kids?"

"Never," my wife answered.

If a mom is lucky, however, she gets to worry just a little less and less all the time as her children grow into fine adults. As the author Dorothy Canfield Fisher wrote right around the time of the first official Mother's Day: "A mother is not a person to lean on, but a person to make leaning unnecessary."

Wise words figuratively, but sometimes literally leaning is a good thing. I say this after recently watching my son, a six-foot-three oak of a young man, lean down and wrap his mom in a cocoon-like hug while resting his chin on the top of her head. Her smile and closed eyes were evidence that every day is a mother's day.

Fifty-Seven

My Little Fellow

———

ABOVE my desk, in a place of honor beside my 2009 Boston Marathon bib, hangs a poem sent to me by John Wooden twenty-six years ago upon the birth of my son. It is titled, "A Little Fellow Follows Me," author unknown, and begins:

> *A careful man I want to be,*
> *A little fellow follows me;*
> *I dare not to go astray,*
> *For fear he'll go the self-same way.*

My little fellow's boyhood bedroom walls were plastered with pictures and posters of Olympic runners Steve Prefontaine and Billy Mills and Deena Kastor. As a second-grader he wrote a poem that also hangs in my office, titled: "I Am A Boy Who Loves To Run."

Today that boy is a six-foot-three young man who still loves to run. Indeed, he was a four-year walk-on and senior captain on the University of Southern California's

Track & Field Team, specializing in the 5,000 meters and the 1,500, and now does his running along the river paths in New York City and in Central Park and in road races.

> *I cannot once escape his eyes,*
> *Whatever he sees me do, he tries;*
> *Like me he says he's going to be,*
> *The little chap who follows me.*

Sharing a run before he left home for his new job with the Clinton Global Initiative in midtown Manhattan, I was reminded of those earlier days of running side by side with the Little Chap Who Follows Me. Running together is still a great way to visit with my son, but maybe even more so when he was very young. We talked a lot. Actually, he did. Me, I mostly listened.

He would tell me about his friends, about school, about his beloved Lakers. Our running conversations also included a lot of questions. Usually his. Often they made me laugh out loud. Like, "Was Gramps really a kid once?"

And, "Is Mom growing shorter?"

Me: "What?"

"Dad, I really think she's shrinking!"

Me (suppressing a laugh): "No, I think you're just growing taller."

"Oh yeah, I guess so."

You can see why I always savored running with The Little Fellow Who Follows Me, even when the pace was slower than I would have liked to keep him from actually following me. Admittedly, I knew this would not last long. Like his shrinking mother, his dad was growing slower.

More than that, The Little Fellow also simply became a faster fellow.

He thinks that I am good and fine,
Believes in every word of mine;
The base in me he must not see,
The little chap who follows me.

I fondly remember one magical day fourteen years ago—it is in my running diary—when The Little Chap Who Follows Me and I went on a three-mile run together. Reaching the turnaround point, I was struggling not to be The Old Man Who Follows Him.

Shortly thereafter, sensing I had fallen behind, he turned around and came back for me. I urged him to go on ahead but this time he ignored every word of mine; he ran alongside me at my pace the rest of the way. I knew this watershed day would arrive, but had thought it was further down the road of life.

I thought wrong. The future had arrived. A couple

days later, midway up "The Long Monster Hill That Makes Your Legs Burn"—as he nicknamed this stretch of asphalt heartbreak—I breathlessly insisted that The Little Fellow Who Follows Me go on ahead to the top.

> *I must remember as I go,*
> *Through summer's sun and winter's snow;*
> *I am building for the years to be*
> *That little chap who follows me.*

With the summer-like sun setting behind the Southern California mountains, I crested the Monster Hill long after The Little Chap Who Follows Me did.

When, at long last, I came into his view, he waved and grinned a big toothy smile that seemed equal parts pride and I-missed-you-Dad. My pride was even greater. It is a mental snapshot I will remember as I go through the rest of my summer suns and winter snows.

Running, of course, is a metaphor. My then-eleven-year-old son's flying Adidas as he effortlessly sailed up The Long Monster Hill That Makes Your Legs Burn and left me behind were a reminder of time's winged flight, that The Little Fellow Who Follows Me would not be little for long.

Figuratively I had glimpsed the future, and it was as it should be. Sons should grow taller and faster and stronger and more talented than their dads. And handsomer and funnier and wiser, too. In short, become better.

Become, also, careful men with their own little fellows who follow them in the years to be.

Until then, The Little Fellow Who Follows Me gets to lead me. And I could not feel more good and fine.

Fifty-Seven

Four Hugs a Day

———

"WE will all go home tonight and give our kids a hug," was a frequent expression from TV news anchors to politicians, parents all, in the first hours following the unspeakable calamity in Newtown, Connecticut.

It was a heartfelt sentiment to be certain. Still, in a way, it added an extra layer to the overwhelming grief and shock. How sad that once again it takes a senseless shooting—I was going to say senseless *tragedy*, but far too often the tragedy is a *shooting*—to put life into a more focused perspective and remind parents to hug their children.

We should never forget to hug our kids.

Two nights after this most recent, and most horrific, shooting—the youth and innocence of twenty of the twenty-seven victims arguably makes it the most horrific to date—my two grown children were home for the holidays. As is our family tradition, they wanted to watch home videos of when they were very young.

It just so happens that the cassette my daughter selected was from when her brother was four and she was six. Through the miracle of a VCR time machine she was exactly like one of the twenty first-graders in Connecticut; Ventura's Poinsettia Elementary could be Sandy Hook Elementary.

Even more so than other American mass shootings, this one has grabbed the heartstrings with clenched fists and refuses to let go. For a human monster to rapidly gun down twenty young children (not to mention seven adults, including the madman's own mother) as though they were merely the pixilated images of a violent video game is unfathomable and makes one's soul weep.

Escaping the newscasts macabre, we hit the "play" button and smiled watching an Easter egg hunt and laughed at my daughter and son's silliness at their birthday parties. Then came tears over words better said—*sang*, actually—by a child than by any adult TV anchor or politician.

My daughter appears on screen, blue-eyed and blond and cute and smiling. In other words she looks just like Emilie Parker, the six-year-old Sandy Hook victim who, as her father tearfully shared with the world, could light up a room, loved to do art and had a remarkable compassionate streak—three traits that similarly make me think of my daughter.

The song my daughter is singing to the video camera is one she had learned the previous year in kindergarten: "Four hugs a day, that's the minimum. Four hugs a day, *not* the maximum..."

The words have remained stuck in my head this past week, although in truth they have been lodged there for the two decades since my daughter first sang them. While I am surely not worthy of the "World's No. 1 Dad" coffee mug I received one distant Father's Day, trying to be the best dad I can has been my top priority eve since I became one.

In this Sisyphean pursuit I have been an extravagant hugger. Four hugs a day? I dare say I routinely dispensed that minimum quota to both kids before they left for school each morning. Even today, as young adults, they cannot avoid my frequent embrace.

Every now and then a young dad or mom will ask me for my single wisest piece of parenting advice. My answer: Hug your kids.

Hug them often. Hug them good morning and goodnight, hello and goodbye, and in between.

Hug them as thanks for a chore well done, as congratulations for a test or art project well done, and also when something done did not go well.

Hug them when they are crying and when they are smiling; when they are toddlers and when they are teens.

Hug them today and tomorrow and every day. Do not allow the hugs to fade until you are reminded by a tragedy to go home and hug your kid tonight.

As the child's song says, "Four hugs a day, that's the minimum. Four hugs a day, *not* the maximum."

Today, in a nod to perspective and remembrance, give twenty hugs.

Fifty-Eight

A City of Two Tales

"IT was the best of times, it was the worst of times."

Charles Dickens was writing about London and Paris in *A Tale of Two Cities*, but on Patriots' Day Monday, 2013, the familiar opening line from his famous novel perfectly described Boston. Indeed, it was a City of Two Tales.

The worst of times was the two evil bombs, designed to kill and maim and cause terror, exploding near the marathon finish line and succeeding on all counts.

But even before the second sinister explosion went off twelve seconds after the first, the best of times were underway. Watching the breaking news videos on TV for the first time, my son saw this best instantly, turning to me and saying: "Look at all the people running *towards* the explosion and going into the fray to help!"

Within three terror-and-adrenaline-fueled-racing heartbeats, the First Responders in bright-colored vests were bravely running *towards* the blast, *towards* the smoke, *towards* the chaos and danger to help victims in an American city suddenly turned into Baghdad or Tel Aviv, into a war zone. Heroic and inspiring fails to describe these actions.

Yet even more remarkable was to see the heroes without vests, the race volunteers and runners and spectators without special emergency and disaster training, hurrying into harm's way to help.

As with 9/11 and Hurricane Sandy and on and on, it was a vivid example of the wisdom of the late Fred Rogers—famously known as Mr. Rogers—who told his children TV viewers that if they saw a scary thing, "Look for the helpers. You will always find people who are helping."

"Helpers" by another word are "heroes."

The best of times was to see images of a burly man "helper" carrying an injured woman away from the blood-wet pavement.

The best of times was to hear a woman praising a "helper" for rushing her to safety in a wheelchair and then racing back to aid another person in need.

The best of times was to learn of a Good Samaritan being, in truth, a Great Samaritan by using his belt as tourniquet to try and save a life; and a runner doing the same with his T-shirt.

The best of times was the marathoners who crossed

the finish line and continued running two more weary miles to Mass General Hospital to donate blood.

The best of times was Patriots Day becoming a day of true patriots.

In the early aftermath the most popular hashtag on Twitter was #PrayforBoston. But people did more than pray—they acted. Restaurants opened and gave free meals; coffee shops provided free Wi-Fi for runners to contact loved ones; on social media message boards local residents offered beds to those who could not return to their hotels.

Feeling a desire to connect in some small way, I posted my own #PrayforBoston tweet: "Today we are all runners."

Even three thousand miles away from all the mayhem in Massachusetts, as a marathon runner myself I soon experienced the outpouring of a unified community. Mere moments after this 21st Century Boston Massacre, a knock came on my front door. It was my concerned neighbor, with whom I have only a wave-in-passing relationship—usually when I am running and he is driving —checking to see if I was home and not racing in Boston.

Too, I received a number of phone calls, texts and e-mails asking the same question. One came from a friend I had not heard from in more than three years; another was from a fellow runner pointing out that the finish-line clock read 4:09 when the blasts went off and, accounting for our delay in the pack of runners getting to the actual starting line of the race four years ago, that is about when we triumphantly ran down Boylston Street—with my wife cheering me on precisely where the second bomb went off.

During a twelve-mile run later on this horrific day, as I tried to settle my thoughts and also honor the victims, three pedestrians—one familiar face and two I did not recognize—yelled out: "Glad you weren't in Boston today."

On Boston Marathon Monday 2013 we were all runners.

More than that, we were all neighbors.

Fifty-Nine

The Healing Wall

—

THE list of sights that have left me briefly speechless is not a long one. In addition to my wife walking down the aisle and my first looks at my newborn daughter and son, the honor roll includes the Grand Canyon and Yosemite Falls as well as such manmade wonders as an Apollo Saturn V rocket and Monet's "Water Lilies" painting.

And, most certainly, the Vietnam Veterans Memorial in Washington, D.C.

It was an unforgettable moment when I rounded the corner at the National Mall in 1983, less than a year after the memorial's completion, and saw the V-shaped wall sunk gracefully into the landscape. Less than a foot high at the two extremities and gently "rising" to more than ten feet at its apex as one walks down an incline towards the center of the mirror-like black marble monument, it is beautiful.

Tragically beautiful. When I visited the memorial again last summer, the experience was no less emotional and overpowering.

Indeed, The Memorial Wall is a 500-foot-long tombstone bearing the names of the 58,267 American Vietnam War servicemen who were either killed in action or remain classified as missing in action.

To put that figure in some small context, 58,000 names fill about 121 white pages in the Oxnard-Camarillo-Ventura phonebook: "A, Raul" through "Gross, Gail." Or this: Dodger Stadium holds 56,000.

The Memorial Wall is commonly called "The Healing Wall" because through the tears it helps release, it provides some solace to loved ones and friends. Visitors make pencil rubbings of the etched names and leave behind notes and love letters, flowers and lighted candles, photographs and mementos.

Too, many will tell you, they leave behind some of their grief. The Healing Wall.

There is a replica memorial called "The Moving Wall" because it has been touring the nation for more than a quarter of a century. The name is further fitting because seeing it is a moving experience. Indeed, while half the size of the original there is nothing diminutive about the tears and emotions The Moving Wall stirs.

Because the names are listed in chronological order, Larry Albert Woodburn is on Panel 05W, Line 80. So far as I know, we are not related. Still, I feel a bond and have learned the Marine from Silver Spring, Maryland was in only his seventh week of duty, in Quang Nam, South Vietnam, when he suffered multiple fragmentation wounds from hostile fire. On February 5, 1971—just eleven days after his twentieth birthday—he was a war casualty.

It is Larry Albert Woodburn who I thought of when I read Tim O'Brien's remarkable 1990 book, *The Things They Carried*, about a platoon of U.S. soldiers in the Vietnam War.

But I also thought about another twenty-year-old kid who fought in those dangerous sweltering jungles. A kid who was a man when I met him. Dave Stancliff.

Dave was the editor of The Twentynine Palms Desert Trail, the first newspaper I worked for after graduating from college. I have had a number of terrific editors and bosses since, but none better. More importantly, I have never worked for, or with, a better person. Tough as a Clint Eastwood character when required, mostly he was a gentleman and a gentle man. War had not hardened his heart. Instead of giving a homeless person a couple bucks for a fast-food hamburger, Dave would buy him a restaurant meal. Or, a greater thing, bring him home for a home-cooked one.

Dave had a run of serious physical health problems related to exposure to the warfare herbicide Agent Orange. The psychological scars were worse. A full night's sleep was rare because of haunting flashbacks. Once, and only once, Dave told me stories about his experience in Vietnam and Cambodia; stories that explained some of The Things *He* Carried internally; stories that gave me nightmares. And he did not even tell me the real hell of it.

If the replica wall comes to your area, I urge you to visit it. Better yet, travel to the National Mall to see the original Vietnam Veterans Memorial. You owe it to the souls whose names are eternally etched upon "The Healing Wall" to give thanks for their ultimate sacrifice. Too, you can honor and give thanks to their fellow soldiers who lived through hell and, by heaven's grace, are not writ upon The Wall.

Thank you, Dave.

Sixty

Hero Among Heroes

———

FOR the first five days of August, I was in the august company of heroes in our nation's capital.

Heroes like astronauts John Glenn and Neil Armstrong and earlier fliers like Charles Lindbergh and the Wright Brothers, all in the Smithsonian National Air and Space Museum.

Men and women heroes interred in Arlington National Cemetery, a heartbreaking landscape that is ironically beautiful.

My tour of heroes included monuments for those who served in World Wars I and II; the Korean War Memorial; and the Vietnam Memorial Wall.

In the National Archives I peered at Founding Father heroes like Benjamin Franklin and John Hancock's faded "John Hancocks" on the original Declaration of Independence.

And, of course, there are the marble heroes in the National Mall: George Washington, Thomas Jefferson,

Abraham Lincoln, Franklin D. Roosevelt and Martin Luther King, Jr.

Yet the hero who arguably engraved the deepest impression on me was one I encountered shortly after my late-night arrival at Ronald Reagan National Airport when I boarded the Metro Blue Line to my downtown D.C. hotel. The first few minutes of the ride were quiet, sans the pleasant rhythmic sounds of the train itself, when suddenly came clamor.

A passenger facing me two rows ahead in the near-empty train car—a tall, sinewy man in his mid-twenties, his bare arms covered with long sleeves of tattoos, his electrocuted blond hair making Einstein's look tame—jumped out of his seat like a jack-in-the-box. He shouted at a goateed man, about the same age as he although shorter and stockier, sitting across the aisle.

Apparently the goateed man had "disrespected" the mangy tattooed man's dog. In a flash the two men were nose-to-nose, although only the tattooed man spoke—or rather, shouted. He cursed at the goateed man; challenged his manhood; unleashed racial taunts. Exclamation marks punctuated his venomous torrent.

At any second I expected weapons to come out and I do not think I was alone; a young woman facing me across the aisle looked absolutely petrified. As the vile racial epithets from the crazed tattooed man intensified, I signaled with my shifting eyes that she—we—should sneak out the exit door at the next stop.

Just then, *THUMP!* The goateed man unloaded a punch. And another. And a third. Frankly, Gandhi might not have blamed him at this point. Meanwhile, the tattooed man's large dog remarkably remained nonviolent.

In slow motion this is what I next witnessed: a bald man with his back to the fray bolted from his seat and in one fluid motion spun 180 degrees into the aisle, took three lightning-quick strides and grabbed the goateed man from behind before he could throw a fourth punch. Breaking apart two pit bulls would have required less courage. It was as if Batman was aboard this Metro car.

Sitting beside his gray-haired wife, the bald man had been as unimposing as Bruce Wayne or a country club golfer: he was wearing peach slacks and a white sweater and appeared old enough to receive Social Security.

Once he rose, however, the Teddy bear came into focus like a grizzly. If not a former NFL linebacker, my guess is he was once an Army sergeant or perhaps a retired police officer for he exuded the authority of both.

After getting between the combatants, who were now both screaming bloodily at each other, the bald man barked commands: "Knock it off! Now! Get out of here! Now! Before you get arrested!"

All the while the bald man strode forward slowly

and wide-footed, a heavyweight boxer backing up a foe, herding the goateed man towards the exit door as a German Shepherd would direct a sheep.

At the next stop the goateed man and tattooed man both got off; the bald man returned to his gray-haired wife's side; and the rest of us in the train car breathed easier.

When my stop came, I used the exit door furthest from me but nearer the bald man.

"Thanks," I said, shaking his hand. "You're a hero."

He smiled humbly, but appreciatively, and almost as widely as did his wife.

Sixty-One

Fab Fours in Granite

———

EIGHT decades ago the sculpture on steroids known as Mount Rushmore had the face of its first rock star dedicated in ceremony. Three years later, in 1936, Thomas Jefferson joined George Washington followed by Abraham Lincoln's face in 1937. Lastly, in 1939, Theodore Roosevelt's spectacled countenance completed the famous presidential quartet.

In honor of the 75th anniversary, I thought it would be fun to consider some other Mount Rushmores. Certainly you will not agree with all—or perhaps even many or any —of my suggestions, but that is part of the fun.

Likely, one's own age and biases will blur their vision. And, hopefully, good-natured arguments will ensue which is fine because these are not written in stone—oh, wait, yes they are!

Let's put the boxing gloves on and begin.

The Mount Rushmore of Boxing: Jack Johnson, Joe Louis, Muhammad Ali, and Rocky Balboa.

The Mount Rushmore of *Sports Illustrated* Swimsuit Models. Surely dating myself, I will go with chiseling in granite these, um, busts: Cheryl Tiegs, Kathy Ireland, Elle Macpherson, and Christie Brinkley.

The Mount Rushmore of American Writers (Male): Hemingway, Twain, Steinbeck and, since this is my list, Jim Murray.

The Mount Rushmore of Writers (Female): Emily Dickinson, J.K. Rowling (for her series of books and their impact on young readers), Maya Angelou (for her voice aloud as well as on the written page), and Dallas Woodburn (tops on *my* list).

The Mount Rushmore of Athletic Shoes: PF Flyers, Chuck Taylor Converse High-Tops, Adidas Superstars, and Nike's original waffle trainers that helped start the running boom in the 1970s.

The Mount Rushmore of Stadiums (since there are far more great stadiums than great presidents, I am breaking this into categories):

Baseball: Yankee Stadium, Fenway Park, Dodger Stadium, and (sorry Wrigley Field) the tiny Field of Dreams.

Football/Track: The Colosseum (in Rome), The Coliseum (Los Angeles Memorial, host of two Olympics and two Super Bowls including the first), The Rose Bowl (framed by the San Gabriel Mountains) and (sorry

Lambeau Stadium, Notre Dame Stadium, Ohio Stadium, Soldier Field and others) The Astrodome (for good reason called in 1965 "The Eighth Wonder of the World").

Arenas: The original Madison Square Garden, the original Boston Garden, The "Fabulous" Forum, and Pauley Pavilion because championship banners matter.

The Mount Rushmore of Cold Cereals: Corn Flakes, Rice Krispies, Raisin Bran, and Wheaties.

My Personal Boyhood Mount Rushmore of Sugar For Breakfast: Froot Loops, Super Sugar Crisp, Alpha-Bits, and Tony The Tiger's "They're *Grrreat!*" Frosted Flakes.

The Mount Rushmore of Candy Bars: Hershey's Bar, Milky Way, Snickers, and 3 Musketeers.

The Mount Rushmore of Basketball: James Naismith (The Inventor), John Wooden (The Wizard), Phil Jackson (The Zen Master) and Jerry West (The NBA's Logo and thus represents all the hardwood greats).

The Mount Rushmore of Quarterbacks: Johnny Unitas, Otto Graham (seven pro championships in ten title games in his ten-year pro career), Joe Montana, and I will have to get back to you on the fourth.

The Mount Rushmore of Tennis (Men)—remember this is my monument: Rod Laver, Bjorn Borg, and Mike and Bob Bryan (unlike the greatest singles player in history, there is no debate over the greatest doubles tandem ever).

The Mount Rushmore of Tennis (Women): Billie

Jean King, Martina Navratilova, Steffi Graf, and Serena Williams.

The Mount Rushmore of Superheroes (Comics): Batman, Superman, Spider-Man, and (my monument) Mighty Mouse.

The Mount Rushmore of Superheroes (Film): John Wayne (almost every role), James Bond, Atticus Finch, and George Bailey.

The Mount Rushmore of inventors: Leonardo da Vinci, Benjamin Franklin, Thomas Edison, and (two-for-one) the Wright Brothers.

The Mount Rushmore of Painters: Vincent van Gogh, Pablo Picasso, Jean-Michel Basquiat (my list), and Greg Woodburn (again, my list).

The Mount Rushmore of Vocalists (Female): Aretha Franklin, Ella Fitzgerald, Janis Joplin, and Whitney Houston.

The Mount Rushmore of Vocalists (Male): I am not even going to try.

The Mount Rushmore of Movies—impossible, but here goes: *The Jazz Singer* (first talkie), *Casablanca* (first on many people's list), *Star Wars*, and (remember it is my list) *It's A Wonderful Life*.

The Mount Rushmore of Rock 'n' Roll: In another impossible category, I go with George, Thomas, Abe and Teddy joined in granite by John, Paul, George, and Ringo.

Sixty-Two

Days of Glory

BRUCE Springsteen's classic "Glory Days" played on the radio earlier today and it got me thinking about athletes who spend their post-playing days looking—and living—in the rearview mirror.

Such as New York Jets quarterback Joe Namath who coolly guaranteed, and more coolly delivered, victory in Super Bowl III against the heavily favored Baltimore Colts in 1969. Three decades later Namath told me: "It was the pinnacle of my life. It was a high I haven't felt or equaled since. If I could be any age again, I would want to stay twenty-five."

And yet staying forever twenty-five would mean he would have missed out later on having his two daughters.

Another Hall of Famer, Bill Bradley, once wrote of retiring from the NBA: "What's left? To live one's days never able to recapture the feeling of those few years of intensified youth."

In other words, even being a U.S. Senator was a letdown from being a young shooting star with the New York Knicks.

"What's left?" How sad to ask this at age twenty-five—or even thirty-five, dotage for most pro athletes.

In the novel *Once a Runner*, John L. Parker, Jr. writes about star athletes "who were (though they didn't realize it at all) at the pinnacle of a life destined to peak so early that the rest if their lives would be a wistful reminiscence of days when poetic deeds were the order of the day."

Similarly, in "Glory Days" Springsteen sings about growing old and sitting back trying to capture the poetic triumphs of his youth that have slipped away, leaving him with nothing but boring stories of those faded glory days.

Fifteen years after his glory days as an All-American high school quarterback, Neely Crenshaw, a character in John Grisham's novel *Bleachers*, returns to his small hometown to visit his old coach who is dying. Crenshaw suffered a career-ending knee injury in college and tells his former teammates: "When you're famous at eighteen, you spend the rest of your life fading away. You dream of the glory days, but you know they're gone forever. I wish I'd never seen a football."

How tragic. Can you imagine a gifted teacher wishing she had never seen a chalkboard; an astronomer lamenting ever touching a telescope; a concert pianist ruing a keyboard?

The night he lost his heavyweight title to Rocky Marciano, Joe Louis was asked whether Rocky punched harder than Max Schmeling had fifteen years earlier, the only other time Louis had been stopped.

"The kid," Louis said of Marciano, "knocked me out with what—two punches? Schmeling knocked me out with—musta been a hundred punches. But I was twenty-two years old. You can take more then than later on."

"Later on" comes far sooner for athletes. A writer, teacher, or architect may not reach the zenith of his or her powers until age fifty or even seventy. Physicians, too, for as Benjamin Franklin noted: "Beware the young doctor."

My dad is not a young doctor. Now eighty-nine, he is still enjoying his glory days saving lives by assisting on cases in the operating room.

"I feel I've always kept improving as a surgeon," Pop shares. "My hands are as steady as ever. What I've lost is the stamina to do long cases. I used to be able to operate all day long, get called back into the hospital that night to do an emergency operation, get two hours of sleep and come back and do it all again the next day. Not anymore. My eyesight is still there, my technical skills are still there, but I don't have a young man's stamina.

"On the other hand, I have continued to gain

knowledge so my decision-making is always improving. Maybe when you are younger, you are more aggressive— sometimes too aggressive. So I think as an older doctor, I'm also a wiser doctor."

John Updike, a highly successful author right up to his death at age seventy-six, once noted, "We all, in a way, peak at eighteen."

My dad disagrees. "I don't think I peaked at eighteen or twenty-five at all," he allows. "I couldn't chose one favorite age I'd want to be because I wouldn't want to have missed everything that came after it. At the time I've lived it, every age has been the best."

That is a glorious attitude.

Sixty-Three

America's Rock of Ages

PRINTED in red letters on a white background, the poster-sized wooden sign reads: "Welcome To The 17th Century."

Meanwhile, twenty yards from where I stood at "Plimouth Plantation"—Plymouth purposely spelled phonetically the way Governor William Bradford did in the 1600s—stood a red vending machine with familiar white script: *Coca-Cola*.

It was a microcosm of my visit to Plymouth, Massachusetts: while trying to step back nearly 400 years in American history, one foot always seemed to remain firmly planted in the 21st Century.

For instance, the *Mayflower II*, a replica of the famous ship the Pilgrims sailed on to America in 1620, is docked beside motorboats, with sleek modern sailboats cruising in the backdrop.

Still, if you narrow your aperture on the full-scale reproduction (about one hundred feet long and twenty-five feet wide), you realize the *Mayflower* was extremely small to carry 102 passengers in the cargo hold—plus thirty crewmen on deck. Indeed, what a cramped, claustrophobic, courageous journey their sixty-six days at sea must have been.

With a dose of imagination, the *Mayflower* comes into focus like a wooden Apollo 11 with two tall masts. Stepping onto Plymouth Rock, as legend claims the Pilgrim party did, was arguably a bigger leap for mankind than Neil Armstrong's first lunar footprint 349 years later. After all, those 102 Pilgrims have an estimated 32 million descendants today while the population on the moon remains zero.

Consider just one passenger, John Howland. It is remarkable the ripples this single settler had on American history. In fact, world events actually hung on the single strand of rope Howland miraculously managed to grab hold of after falling overboard during a storm midway through the voyage.

Because Howland was rescued from the frigid Atlantic waters, he completed the journey; was one of fifty-one Pilgrims to survive the first winter of illness and hunger; and ultimately had more descendants than any of his fellow passengers.

Moreover, his descendants include U.S. presidents Franklin D. Roosevelt and both George Bushes. Also, literature's Henry Wadsworth Longfellow and Ralph

Waldo Emerson. None of these important figures would have been born had Howland perished before grabbing that fateful towline.

Leo Martin, a renowned historian, was our guide for a foot tour of all things Pilgrim. He dressed the part, wearing a brown felt hat and matching shirt with laces at the neck, tan knickers, red stockings and—*Coca-Cola*-like juxtaposition—modern walking shoes.

The two-hour field trip was far more fascinating than the classroom lectures of my youth. One nugget: Leo noted that Bradford brought 400 books on the *Mayflower*— more volumes than Harvard College had when it was founded in 1636.

While the Pilgrim colony library was large, Plymouth Rock is not. Indeed, it underwhelms many largely because it is so small. Originally fifteen feet long, three feet wide, and weighing ten tons, what remains visible on shore today is only about the size of a queen mattress.

No matter. "The Great Rock" still gave me goose bumps.

Plymouth Rock rests inside a steel cage, like a zoo animal almost, to protect it from thieves who would chip off souvenir chunks. Five feet above, at street level, the sacred site is surrounded by a beautiful open-air outdoor columned structure resembling a Roman temple.

A piece of Plymouth Rock is on display a few blocks away in Pilgrim Hall, America's oldest continuously operating museum. Rubbing the stone is said to bring good luck, much like kissing Ireland's Blarney Stone promises the gift of eloquence: I remain hopeful still of receiving both rewards.

Too, I have rubbed a tiny slice of moon rock in the Smithsonian's National Air and Space Museum and, honestly, touching America's Rock of Ages was an equal thrill. After all, if the story of Plymouth Rock is true and not apocryphal, then this modest boulder is the symbolic "ground zero" for 21st Century America.

"I believe the Pilgrims did step on Plymouth Rock," Leo told me, and I choose to believe him. As Hemingway wrote in *The Sun Also Rises*: "Isn't it pretty to think so?"

Sixty-Four

Authors Ridge

———

SIXTY miles north of Plymouth Rock, I made a pilgrimage to another "ground zero" in American history: the Old North Bridge in Concord, Mass., where the Revolutionary War erupted on April 19, 1775.

The replica bridge, like Plymouth Rock, proved much smaller in person than anticipated. Also, similarly, it made my imagination whirl as I surveyed the landscape, my sight rising from the Concord River to the high ground where the Minute Men held the advantage.

Surprisingly, a different ridge proved to be a higher highlight for me.

On our rental-car drive to the Old North Bridge, my wife and I made a short detour to Sleepy Hollow Cemetery. Specifically, to the upper area near the back called "Authors Ridge."

It is a fitting name because on this picturesque-as-a-thousand-words tree-shaded ridge, all within an acorn's toss of each other, are the graves of four significant 19th

Century American authors: Nathaniel Hawthorne, Louisa May Alcott, Ralph Waldo Emerson and Henry David Thoreau. Call it Ridge Rushmore.

First up is the Thoreau family plot which has a shared monument stone the size of a chest of drawers bearing the names, birthdates and dates of death of parents John and Cynthia D., as well as their offspring John Jr., Helen L., Henry D. (Born July 12, 1817, Died May 6, 1862) and Sophia E.

Surrounding the monument are six small headstones, each barely bigger than a hardcover book, reading: Mother, Father, Sophia, John, Helen and …

… Henry.

How perfect this is, for as he famously advised during his life: "Simplify, simplify." No dates. No full name. Simply "HENRY" in all caps.

Modest be it, Henry's marker readily stands out for it is decorated like a Christmas tree, albeit instead of with ornaments and lights it is adorned with a classroom's worth of pens and pencils of various colors leaning against it, some with messages and names—"Thank You" and "Bless You" and "Anna" and "Steven" on this day—written on them by worshipers who made the pilgrimage to pay homage.

Originally, I left behind a pen but quickly thought the better of it and instead balanced a yellow No. 2 pencil—

after writing "Simplify" and "Woody" on it—for Thoreau was also a renowned pencil maker in addition to being a writer, poet, philosopher, naturalist, and surveyor.

The headstone for the author of *The Scarlet Letter* is slightly larger than Henry's marker, and rests upon a pedestal, yet it too is simple, reading only: Hawthorne. It also has a few pens left at its base, as well as coins and stones balanced upon its arched top.

A flat rectangular stone, whitened by the elements and flush to the ground, marks the grave of Louisa M. Alcott, author of *Little Women*. A Union nurse during the Civil War, Alcott's grave also has a small American flag, the sort a child might wave curbside at a Fourth of July parade, with a "U.S. Veteran" medallion on its staff. Expectedly, the site is graced with a collection of pencils and pens.

Ralph Waldo Emerson's gravestone, meanwhile, is a refrigerator-sized hunk of beautiful raw granite. Attached is a copper plaque, long ago having turned a handsome green patina, decorated with four flowers on top and below reading: "Ralph Waldo Emerson / Born in Boston May 25 1803 / Died in Concord April 27 1882."

Lastly, the plaque quotes this line from his poem "The Problem"—"The passive Master lent his hand / To the vast soul that o'er him planned."

The problem of where to place pens and pencils to

honor the word master Emerson has been solved by admirers who have wedged pennies and dimes between the plaque and granite, some of the coins at 90-degree angles to form mini-shelves. So it was I balanced the pen originally intended for Thoreau's marker.

Leaving "Authors Ridge," breathtaking in both its beauty and literary hallowedness, this line from Thoreau came fittingly to mind: "Heaven is under our feet as well as over our heads."

Sixty-Five

Walden Pond

———

WE begin where I left off in the previous essay: "Heaven is under our feet as well as over our heads."

This quote by Henry David Thoreau aptly describes "Authors Ridge," where he, Louisa May Alcott, Nathaniel Hawthorne, and Ralph Waldo Emerson rest in shaded peace beneath picturesque woods in Sleepy Hollow Cemetery in Concord, Massachusetts.

Too, his sentiment beautifully depicts a scene less than two miles away, south on Walden Street through town, passing Emerson Playground and Thoreau Street, and then a bit further.

Two miles by car—and seemingly 200 years by calendar.

Indeed, this summer past marked the 170th anniversary of Thoreau's celebrated experiment in self-examination and independence that began in July of 1845.

"I went to the woods because I wished to live deliberately, to front only the essential facts of life,"

Thoreau wrote in his transcendent treatise, *Walden, or Life in the Woods*, which was not published until 1854, eight years before his death at age forty-four. "And to see if I could not learn what it had to teach and not, when I came to die, discover that I had not lived."

Visiting where Thoreau lived for two years, two months and two days in a one-room cabin he self-reliantly built—at a frugal cost of $28.12—is to see those pages brought to life.

This author's ridge, among pitch pines and hickories, is more gorgeous than I had imagined. Conjure up the most scenic pond you have ever seen, multiply that loveliness threefold, and still you will come up short of the view of Walden Pond below.

Unlike Plymouth Rock and the Old North Bridge, both being much smaller than anticipated, Walden Pond in person is grander. It seems more a lake.

The cabin, which measured ten feet by fifteen feet with two windows—and held a bed, small table, desk and two chairs—is long gone. It was dismantled for scrap lumber, just as the *Mayflower*, I learned earlier in this trip, was used to build homes after its return voyage from Plymouth to England.

The cabin site—specifically, the second-hand chimney bricks—was discovered in 1945, the centennial of the start of Thoreau's retreat. Today, nine square granite posts, each about four feet tall and connected by a chain, mark the outline of the cabin.

A few paces to the side is a rock pile, perhaps twenty feet square. It began modestly in 1872 when Bronson Alcott, a lifelong friend of Thoreau, visited Walden Pond and placed a few stones to mark the cabin's location. Ever since, admirers and disciples from the world over have extended the tradition.

Walt Whitman came in 1881, writing afterwards: "I too carried one and deposited on the heap." John Muir did likewise, twice, in 1883 and 1893.

I now belong in the company of Whitman and Muir.

Some making the pilgrimage embellish their tributes with Thoreau quotes. "The price of anything is the amount of life you exchange for it," was printed in black marker on a triangular stone I saw.

In chalk, a round stone read: "breathe deeply + live wildly."

A book cover-sized flat stone was filled fully: "Most men lead lives of quiet desperation and go to the grave with the song still in them."

Reflecting on Thoreau's song, I considered how these nuggets would fit nicely in 140-character Tweets— and yet how appalled he would surely be by Twitter, by texting, by our un-simplified modern world where the masses seem too distracted by consumerism to live wildly.

"Go confidently in the direction of your dreams. Live the life you've imagined. – H. D. Thoreau," read another stone in the pile.

One more: "Our life is frittered away by detail. Simplify, simplify."

But here was my favorite rock lyric: "Thoreau's mom did his laundry."

Indeed, it is true. Thoreau regularly broke his contemplative solitude with a half-hour walk to his parents' home to enjoy his mother's apple pies and—time out from self-reliance—he would bring his dirty clothes.

Sixty-Six

Smiling Side-Trip

——

THE loveliness of Walden Pond in person is threefold beyond expectations, but eighty miles southwest—as Sammy Jay flies—I happened upon a small body of water that not only rivals Henry David Thoreau's famous basin, but lives up to its own name: The Smiling Pool.

Most likely you are not familiar with Sammy Jay and his fellow characters who lived in, and played near, The Smiling Pool and neighboring Old Briar Patch in *The Bedtime Story-Books* series written by Thornton W. Burgess beginning in 1910.

But the various "Adventures of" Jimmy Skunk, Grandfather Frog, Old Man Coyote, Bobby Raccoon, Jerry Muskrat, Buster Bear and a menagerie of forest friends wearing clothes were my dad's favorite stories in the 1930s; mine in the '60s; and, in turn, my daughter's and sons' most-requested in the early 1990s. The tattered book jackets and finger-worn pages of twenty hardcover editions reveal how often they have been reread.

Sometimes you take a trip and other times, I believe, a trip takes you. The latter is often better.

After my wife and I were shown the *Mayflower* Society House, where pilgrim descendant Ralph Waldo Emerson was married, in Plymouth, Massachusetts; then unexpectedly stumbled upon "Authors' Ridge" where Emerson, Nathaniel Hawthorne, Louisa May Alcott and Thoreau are eternal neighbors in Sleepy Hollow Cemetery in Concord; followed by a visit to nearby Walden Pond, it was apparent an "author" theme had grabbed our road map.

So it was that in Cape Cod I serendipitously learned the Thornton W. Burgess Society Museum was in nearby East Sandwich. A side trip beckoned me like Chatterer The Red Squirrel is drawn to a pile of acorns.

Burgess, who was born in 1874, is certainly not as acclaimed as the Fab Four at Author's Ridge. However, during the first half of the 20th Century, it was claimed at the museum, he was as popular as Sesame Street is today.

By the time of his death at age ninety, Burgess authored more than 170 books and had 16,000 stories syndicated in newspapers across the country. His work was also published around the world in French, Spanish, German, Italian, Swedish and Gaelic.

And yet "The Bedtime Story-Man" was far more than a children's author. He was a popular figure on radio from 1912 to 1960, including a show about nature.

Indeed, Burgess was at heart a conservationist. He collaborated on a series of books that proved instrumental in the growth of a fledging organization created in 1910—The Boy Scouts of America. Too, he helped found bird sanctuaries and in 1918 successfully lobbied Congress to pass the Migratory Bird Act.

His legacy lives on in the non-profit educational Thornton W. Burgess Society with the mission: "To inspire reverence for wildlife and concern for the natural environment." He wrote his bedtime stories with the same goal.

Housed in a two-centuries-old home that overlooks The Smiling Pool—looking down at it from a hill the curved pond resembles a smile—and Old Briar Patch of Thornton's youth, the museum also features Green Briar Nature Center; Briar Patch Conservation Area; and Green Briar Jam Kitchen, America's oldest commercial jam kitchen dating back to 1903 and still looks in its original design, where school children see fruit preserves made without preservatives.

There is also, of course, a writing wing. To see hundreds of rare-edition Thornton Waldo Burgess books, some familiar to my eyes, was a time machine back to both my childhood and my early parenthood.

Outside, admiring the Smiling Pool, my trip's

author theme intensified as a quote from the other wordsmith Waldo—Ralph Waldo Emerson—came to mind: "Live in the sunshine, swim the sea, drink the wild air."

I smiled, imaging Buster Bear and Reddy Fox doing exactly that below.

In the closing paragraph of each bedtime book, Burgess tells the reader what adventure he will write about next. This especially made sense because his books originated as serialized newspaper stories.

And so, because a four-essay serial has proved insufficient for my Eastern Seaboard adventure, we will pick up from here with a bonus chapter to follow.

Sixty-Seven

Reflecting on an Adventure

———

THE Smiling Pool, from the children's books by Thornton Burgess, is aptly named because viewed from atop an overlooking hill—as Burgess did often during his boyhood in East Sandwich, Massachusetts—its curved shape resembles a smile. Indeed, it remains a happy place to sojourn.

My emotions were completely polar at the next pool of water I visited. Actually, pools plural: the twin reflecting pools at the National September 11 Memorial in lower Manhattan. The Crying Pools seems apropos.

Each reflecting pool is nearly an acre square situated on the footprints where the Twin Towers majestically stood. Water pours over all four edges of each pool at a rate of 3,000 gallons per minute, forming waterfall curtains, before disappearing down a small square abyss at the bottom.

The symbolism of the flow rate is heart numbing because nearly 3,000 lives disappeared in the terrorist attacks of September 11, 2001 and February 26, 1993. These victims' names are inscribed on bronze panels on the parapets surrounding the pools. The result is to turn many eyes into miniature reflecting pools overflowing with tears.

This was my first return to the site since Tuesday, June 11, 2002—nine months to the day after the World Trade Center became Ground Zero. I know this because I still have my "WTC:00 Viewing Platform—2:00-2:30 pm" ticket.

I remember very little from those NBA Finals I covered, other than the Lakers played the Nets, but the sight of the steep-sided square hole in the ground remains unforgettable. It looked like a gargantuan grave.

Inside the 9/11 Memorial Museum the somberness is even more overwhelming than at the twin reflecting pools. Boxes of tissues are placed liberally throughout yet short lines still form. My wife teared up within the first two minutes of entering the exhibition. She had lasted longer than I.

To tour the museum *once* is a must, I believe; I believe also I could not bear to do so again.

To describe the experience would require a dozen essays. Instead, I will share a single image that most profoundly affected me. It is the transcript of a phone call from Brian Sweeney, a thirty-eight-year-old passenger aboard United Airlines Flight 175, to his wife. Julie wasn't home, so he left his last words on their answering machine:

"Jules, this is Brian. Listen, I'm on an airplane that's been hijacked. If things don't go well, and it's not looking good, I just want you to know I absolutely love you. I want you to do good. Go have a good time. Same to my parents and everybody. And I just totally love you and I'll see you when you get there. Bye, babe. I'll try to call you."

At 9:03 a.m. the plane crashed into the South Tower.

As I wrote in this series previously, this trip took on an "author" theme with Ralph Waldo Emerson, Henry David Thoreau, Louisa May Alcott, Nathaniel Hawthorne and Thornton W. Burgess playing roles.

However, I believe Brian Sweeney's words— composed with no time for writer's block, no chance to edit and polish them—are as potent and poignant as any left behind by the above masters.

After telling my son to do good, have a good time and that I absolutely love him, I hugged him goodbye while battling to keep my twin reflecting pools of green from overflowing, my heart buoyed in knowing he has settled into New York City quickly, made friends, likes his new job, and is enjoying this exciting chapter in his life.

On the plane home, a quote from one more author —J.F.K. wrote the 1957 Pulitzer Prize-winning *Profiles in Courage*—came back to mind. I had seen it earlier in our trip at the John F. Kennedy Hyannis Museum in Cape Cod:

"I always go to Hyannisport to be revived, to know again the power of the sea and the Master who rules over it and us."

This is how I always feel returning to Ventura.

Sixty-Eight

A Few Things I Know

——

AFTER blowing out enough birthday candles to grill dinner over, here are a few things I have come to know…

Despite all the great things said about them, dogs are still underrated.

Chocolate is overrated. Just kidding.

Don't save the good china for special occasions only.

People, not things, matter.

Batteries in a smoke detector only get low enough to cause ear-piercing warning *BEEPS!* in the middle of the night, never during the day.

The final twenty-five percent of power in a cell phone battery goes ten times faster than the first seventy-five percent.

Never pass up a chance to look at the ocean, a sunrise or sunset, stars on a clear night or a masterpiece painting such as *Starry Night*.

Breaking bread together really does help break

down barriers.

You will pretty much never regret spending money to travel—even a "bad" trip will give you some good memories to last a lifetime.

Robert Frost was right: take the road less traveled by.

The hassles of air travel—security lines, flight delays, lack of leg room, et cetera—are greatly overemphasized when you consider how miraculous it is that you can pretty much decide on a destination in the morning and be anywhere in America by this evening or in the world by tomorrow.

Travel by Clipper ship, Conestoga wagon or even a Model T, now those had hassles.

Who you travel with is far more important than *where* you travel.

Spend as much time as you can with people who lift you up and as little as possible with those who pull you down.

Double-knot your shoelaces.

A good friend surprises you with a nice deed. A rare and great friend does a nice deed that surprises you—until you think for a moment and realize you are not really surprised at all.

Procrastination is not one of the seven deadly sins so do not beat yourself up over it—at least not until tomorrow.

Batman is the greatest of all superheroes. Well, behind moms.

Call me old-fashioned, but I think guys shouldn't wear hats indoors and should open doors for women.

James M. Barrie, author of *Peter Pan*, was right: "Those who bring sunshine into the lives of others, cannot keep it from themselves."

Roller coasters and high diving boards are more thrilling when you are a kid—but just barely.

A lot of movies are longer than they should be and most hugs are too short.

The experts who say you cannot be your kid's friend, even when they are young, are dead wrong. That's my experience anyway.

If you can choose one thing to be world class at, make it the fine art of friendship.

The African proverb is right: "There are two lasting gifts you can give your child: one is roots, the other is wings."

Writing a thank-you note is always a few minutes well spent.

Kindness is more powerful than penicillin.

It is not really a favor if you make the recipient feel like you are doing a favor.

My friend and mentor Wayne Bryan is right: "If

you don't make an effort to help others less fortunate than you, then you're just wasting your time on Earth."

A positive attitude will positively carry you a long way.

It takes worn-out running shoes to finish a marathon; worn-out brushes before you can paint a masterpiece; and well-worn pots and pans to create a seasoned chef.

"Like" is, um, like, an overworked word; "love" an underused one.

Gratitude is an underworked emotion.

Maya Angelou was right: "When you leave home, you take home with you." Also, "Try to be the rainbow in somebody's cloud."

John Wooden was right about most things, including: "Things turn out best for those who make the best of the way things turn out"; "Study and work hard, but make time for play too"; and, "Make each day your masterpiece."

We should all make a wish and blow out a candle 365 times a year because every day is a once-in-a-lifetime experience to be celebrated.

Sixty-Nine

A Wonderful Mess

———

HERE is a surprising statistic I recently came across: approximately thirty percent of Americans cannot fit their car—or cars—into their garage.

I say "surprising" because thirty percent seems far too low. Indeed, I thought the "Ninety-Nine Percenters" referred to the overwhelming majority of people whose garages are filled with so many bicycles, bats, balls, beach chairs, boxes and more boxes, even billiard tables and boats —and this is just the short list of stuff starting with the letter B—to actually park a BMW or Buick in there too.

Shoehorning the entire alphabet of things inside a two*-car garage can leave no room for even a single subcompact, much less an SUV. This is despite the fact that over the past two decades the average American garage has nearly doubled in size and the number of three*-car garages has increased sixty percent.

(* These numerical terms are theoretical. In reality, one must subtract one car from the stated vehicle occupancy of a garage to arrive at the realistic figure.)

Personally, our home has a two*-car garage by which I of course mean we have a one-car garage. At least there was a time when we could fit a single car inside. In fact, I am proud to say passengers on either side could even open a door to get in and out.

After a while, however, like parking between two civilian tanks (pronounced "SUVs") that are both in spaces marked "Compact Only," it became necessary to let everyone on the passenger side of the car get out before pulling in.

And then a few years ago our two*-car garage became a zero-car Self Storage Unit.

The major, but by no means lone, culprit was the Mount Whitney-sized pile of running shoes our son collected through his nonprofit organization Give Running to send to kids living in impoverished villages and orphanages in developing countries as well as disadvantaged American communities. You might reasonably assume that after he and I filled a rented cargo van with more than 800 pairs of sneakers one weekend, and dropped them off to be shipped overseas to Africa, that upon our return home there would have once again been room in the garage for at least a Honda Civic.

And, yes, there would have been... except that we returned with the van sardine-packed with such cargo as a bed, dresser, desk and the rest of the contents from his apartment at graduate school.

Make no mistake, it was wonderful having the newly minted MBA grad home for most of the summer as a "Boomerang Kid" before he left for a dream job in New York City. My worry, however, was that our garage would remain filled with all of his "Boomerang Booty" after he moved back out. My fears proved true—his furniture remains in storage in our garage. Add to that running shoe donations that still come in before they go out, and both our cars must park in the driveway.

Meanwhile, over the summer the inside of our formerly empty nest similarly looked like a tornado had passed through with more of our son's belongings tossed about alongside those of our daughter, who was back home visiting from the Bay Area for a few weeks.

All this mayhem and mess should have been enough to drive my wife a little crazy and to be counting down the days until life around here returned to normal. That was not the case, however, because this was the "normal" we prefer. Indeed, it was a magical summer to savor. We would not trade that chaos of clutter for cleared countertops and mess-free tables and a spotless two*-car garage that really can hold two cars.

When both kids were very young, I clipped out a Family Circus cartoon from the Sunday newspaper and it adorned our refrigerator door for well over a decade until it finally disintegrated beyond repair by Scotch Tape. But the images remain preserved in my mental flash drive. The first of two panels showed the mom looking at a huge mess of toys strewn around the otherwise empty room and wishfully thinking: "When will these things all be put away?"

In the second panel, Billy, Dolly, Jeffy and P.J.'s mom images herself having grown gray while wistfully looking at the same toys that are now put away and gathering cobwebs in the attic.

With the American Girl Dolls and Power Ranger action figures long ago boxed up in our shrinking garage, my wife and I always relish the new fleeting times when our kids' things are not put away.

Seventy

Masterpiece Resolutions

"NEW Year's is a harmless annual institution," wrote Mark Twain, "of no particular use to anybody save as a scapegoat for promiscuous drunks, and friendly calls, and humbug resolutions, and we wish you to enjoy it with a looseness suited to the greatness of the occasion."

In addition to wishing you and yours a New Year filled with great joy and health, I thought I would take a moment before December's calendar page turns to January to make some resolutions—humbug and laudable both. Perhaps you will find some worthy of your own pursuit. I resolve to ...

... keep in mind the words of Ralph Waldo Emerson, who wrote: "Write it on your heart that every day is the best day in the year. He is rich who owns the day, and no one owns the day who allows it to be invaded with fret and anxiety."

... own my day.

... try to live up to the wisdom of these lines in

Rudyard Kipling's remarkable poem "If"—"If you can meet with Triumph and Disaster / And treat those two imposters just the same."

... try to treat Fret and Anxiety like the imposters they are.

... unplug, unplug, unplug.

... sunscreen, sunscreen, sunscreen.

... pass up the nearest open parking spot in order to leave it for someone, perhaps an elderly person, who might find it difficult to walk very far.

... give compliments one hundred times more frequently than unsolicited advice.

... not count the items in a person's crowded basket in front of me at the Ten Items Or Less Express Line. It is not like an extra three or five items of theirs is going to delay me terribly.

... listen to more live music—the smaller the venue the better.

... listen to others more—and more closely.

... laugh more—including at myself.

... try to, as my hero Coach John Wooden encouraged and practiced, "Make friendship a fine art."

... try to, as Eleanor Roosevelt advised, "Do one thing every day that scares you." Or, at least, challenges you.

... heed Samuel Beckett's wisdom to "Try again.

Fail again. Fail better."

... try to suffer fools more gladly. As my Grandpa Ansel said, "It is good at times to deal with ignorant people because it makes you feel so smart."

... try not to be an ignorant fool too often myself.

... again from Grandpa Ansel, keep in mind: "The only way to travel life's road is to cross one bridge at a time."

... again from Coach Wooden: "Read deeply from good books."

... read shallowly from fun books, too.

... use my car horn as though I have to pay $10 for each honk.

... buy at least *two* of anything a kid under age ten is selling.

... check my email in-box less frequently and write more snail-mail letters.

... spend less time on Facebook and more time face-to-face with people who enrich my spirit.

... conserve water.

... shop at local small businesses first, local chains second, and buy online as a last resort.

... pick up litter and not just on Beach Clean-Up Days.

... keep a coffee-chain gift card in my wallet for when I come across someone down-on-their-luck.

... stop to smell the roses—and daydream at the clouds, and savor sunsets, and marvel at starry night skies, and appreciate similar works of nature's art.

... visit more museums.

... heed John Muir's call to "Keep close to nature's heart and break clear away, once in a while, and climb a mountain or spend a week in the woods. Wash your spirit clean."

... be quicker to forgive.

... be slower to criticize—others and myself.

... give flowers out of the blue and not just to mark special occasions.

Lastly, with my favorite Wooden-ism in mind, I resolve in the New Year to try to "Make each day a masterpiece."

Seventy-One

Masterpiece, Day by Day

——

DEAR Class of 2016, I am honored to have been invited (albeit by myself) to address you here today.

Michelangelo, when asked how he had created one of his masterpiece sculptures, replied simply: "I saw the angel in the marble and carved until I set him free."

Creating your own masterpiece life, dear graduates, as you journey forward requires a similar process: you must see the angel—your passion—and then set it free.

For Michelangelo, this meant chipping away the pieces of marble that did not look like the angel or the horse or David. In our lives, this means chipping away the distractions and challenges and even chipping away the negative people who are preventing us from achieving our dreams.

In addition to being sculptors, you are also painters who create your masterpiece by adding brushstrokes of color to the canvas. In other words, by adding determination and patience and love to your life's palette, to name just three key hues.

For good reason my dear mentor and hero John Wooden advised focusing on creating your masterpiece *day* and not your masterpiece *life*. A masterpiece sculpture is created one chisel strike at a time; a masterpiece painting one brushstroke at a time; a masterpiece novel one keystroke at a time; a masterpiece wall, one brick at a time. So is a masterpiece life—private and professional—created one masterful day at a time, one after another, until they add up to masterpiece weeks, months, years.

To focus on a masterpiece life, or even a masterpiece year, is too daunting. Better to keep in mind this piece of wisdom from Coach Wooden: "Little things add up to big things."

Masterpiece days add up to masterpiece decades.

A parable about a starfish emphasizes the big power of little acts. It was a beautiful Southern California morning and a beachcomber was walking along the sand that was littered with kelp and driftwood from a violent storm the night before. In the distance he noticed a man bend down to pick something up and then toss it into the ocean.

Every few steps, the man repeated this calisthenic: stop, bend, stand, toss. But what was he throwing, the beachcomber wondered: Driftwood sticks? Broken seashells? Skipping stones?

As the two morning walkers neared each other, the beachcomber finally realized the man was picking up starfish that, by the hundreds, had been washed ashore by the violent storm's high surf and left stranded.

The beachcomber could not help but laugh at the other man's futile efforts. "You're just wasting your time," he said. "There are too far many starfish for you to make a difference before they die."

"Maybe," the man replied as he gently tossed another starfish into the waves. "But to this one I'm making a world of difference."

As you venture out into the world, Class of 2015, keep an eye out for "starfish" who need your help.

Before closing, I would like to share a passage near the end of Ray Bradbury's classic novel, *Fahrenheit 451*: "Everyone must leave something behind when he dies, my grandfather said. A child or a book or a painting or a house or a wall built or a pair of shoes made. Or a garden planted. Something your hand touched some way so your soul has somewhere to go when you die, and when people look at that tree or that flower you planted, you're there."

These words remind me of a poem by my grandfather Ansel, handwritten on the title page of his medical college textbook *Modern Surgery* and dated Oct. 1, 1919, less than a year before Bradbury was born:

> *The worker dies, but the work lives on*
> *Whether a picture, a book, or a clock*
> *Ticking the minutes of life away*
> *For another worker in metal or rock*
> *My work is with children and women and men —*
> *Not iron, not brass, not wood*
> *And I hope when I lay my stethoscope down*
> *That my Chief will call it good.*

By finding your passion and the work that you want to live on, dear graduates, and by creating your masterpiece day, over and again, in the end your Chief will call it good.

Acknowledgements

———

IT took John Wooden fourteen years to complete his famous Pyramid of Success—after all, "Good things take time, usually *a lot* of time"—as he kept rearranging the blocks and revising the wording until he felt he had it just right. As evidence, one single word in the block "Team Spirit" frustrated him for much of that span; Coach had said there must be a "willingness" to help teammates and the team, but finally realized the precise word he wanted was "eagerness."

The wisdom in this small change resonated numerous times with me while working on *Strawberries in Wintertime*.

For example, I remember asking my son if he could help me create my Kickstarter video when he got a chance in the next few days. Even though Greg was in full concentration in his art loft upstairs, his immediate reply was not a *willingness* to help me when he finished his painting session, but instead an enthusiastic, "You bet, Pop!

Let's do it now!" His *eagerness,* then as usual, made my heart soar.

A similar scene played out, almost word for word, when I asked my daughter, Dallas, if she would edit the written content for my Kickstarter campaign webpage: "Of course, Dad! I'd love to!"

Dallas' and Greg's eagerness to assist me with their many talents throughout the remainder of this journey—from social media to cover design, from copyediting the entire manuscript to final print layout—not only has made *Strawberries in Wintertime* a better book, but made the endeavor so very enjoyable. Indeed, I cannot thank my two remarkable children/best-friends/role-models—for a role model need not be an elder—enough for being in this anthology as frequent essay subjects and also in each page as my collaborators. As with *Wooden & Me*, Dallas and Greg have turned this laborious undertaking into a lovely experience.

Speaking of lovely, words fall far shy in expressing proper thanks to my wife, Lisa—who I fittingly met in wintertime—for filling my Life with Love and Laugher.

Special gratitude goes to my sister, Kym, who vowed to pledge the entire fund-raising goal needed for publication, if need be, to make *Strawberries in Wintertime* a reality.

My sincere thanks also extend to everyone who

eagerly supported *Strawberries in Wintertime* on Kickstarter. And I do mean every single person because the funding goal was surpassed by a mere twelve dollars, which means that *literally* every one of you was the *deciding* patron to success! By the way, success came with just nine minutes to spare before the deadline and a full one-third of the funding goal was pledged in the final twelve hours of the three-week campaign. That is an "eagerness to help" that would make John Wooden smile. So thank you, all, for making me feel a bit like George Bailey in the closing scene of *It's A Wonderful Life* as you were my fellow townspeople (near and far, brought close by the Internet) rallying to my aid.

Always, when I have the chance, I must thank the late Jim Murray for inspiring me to become a writer in the first place and later befriending me. Similarly, my deep gratitude lives on for Coach John Wooden's friendship and mentorship—his wisdom and lasting impact on my life are readily apparent in many of the essays in these pages.

My sincere and ongoing gratefulness also goes to the wondrous Bryans—Kathy and Wayne, Bob and Mike—whose unyielding support, guidance, and friendship remains priceless to Dallas, Greg, Lisa, and me. Here is a measure of my esteem for Wayne: he has been the matching bookend of Coach Wooden in my life—first as my youth tennis coach; in adulthood as a friend and mentor; and always as a role model.

Because of the eagerness from so many to offer their support, *Strawberries in Wintertime* has come to life in print. If you read *Wooden & Me*, the following words from Coach to me will be familiar—but that does not make them any less heartfelt as I express them to you: "Although it is often used without true feeling, when it is used with sincerity, no collection of words can be more expressive or meaningful than the very simple word—Thanks!"

About the Author

WOODY Woodburn has been an award-winning journalist for more than three decades, including twenty-five years as a sports columnist in Southern California with *The Ventura County Star* and then *The South Bay Daily Breeze* in Torrance. He is again writing for *The Star* in Ventura, now as a general interest essayist. His newspaper career had earlier stops in Santa Maria, Paso Robles, Twentynine Palms, and Santa Barbara.

National recognition for Woodburn includes First Place for Column Writing by the Associated Press News Executive Council; Column Writing honors by the Associated Press Sports Editors; E.W. Scripps Newspapers "Columnist of the Year" and Copley News Service's "Columnist of the Year"; and the James S. Copley "Ring of Truth" award. In 2003, Woodburn was inducted into the Jim Murray Memorial Foundation's Journalists Hall of Fame. In 2015, Woodburn was inducted into the Ventura County Sports Hall of Fame.

Woodburn's writing has appeared in *The Best American Sports Writing* anthology; *The Sporting News*; and more than a dozen *Chicken Soup For The Soul* anthologies, both sports-themed and non-sports related.

Woodburn authored the highly acclaimed memoir *Wooden & Me* in 2013, and co-authored *Raising Your Child To Be A Champion In Athletics, Arts and Academics* in 2004 with nationally renowned speaker and coach Wayne Bryan.

Woodburn's community involvement includes his annual "Woody's Holiday Ball Drive" that to date has collected more than $100,000 worth of new sports balls for underprivileged youth.

Woody lives in Ventura, California, with his wife, Lisa; the couple has been married for thirty-three years and has two adult children—daughter, Dallas, a novelist living in the Bay Area, and son, Greg, who works for the Clinton Global Initiative in New York City.

Woody can be contacted through his website: woodywoodburn.com.

Made in the USA
San Bernardino, CA
10 January 2016